Mapping the World
of
Harry Potter

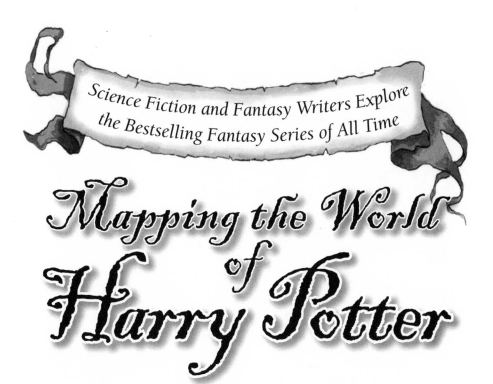

Science Fiction and Fantasy Writers Explore the Bestselling Fantasy Series of All Time

Mapping the World of Harry Potter

EDITED BY

Mercedes Lackey

WITH

LEAH WILSON

BENBELLA

BENBELLA BOOKS, INC.
Dallas, Texas

BenBella Books, Inc.
6440 N. Central Expressway, Suite 617
Dallas, TX 75206
www.benbellabooks.com
Send feedback to feedback@benbellabooks.com

Printed in the United States of America
10 9 8 7 6 5 4 3 2 1

Library of Congress Cataloging-in-Publication Data

Mapping the world of Harry Potter : science fiction and fantasy writers
explore the bestselling fantasy series of all time / edited by Mercedes
Lackey, with Leah Wilson.
     p. cm.
     ISBN 1-932100-59-8
     1. Rowling, J. K.--Criticism and interpretation. 2. Fantasy fiction,
English—History and criticism. 3. Children's stories, English—History
and criticism. 4. Rowling, J. K.—Characters—Harry Potter. 5. Potter,
Harry (Fictitious character) 6. Wizards in literature. 7. Magic in
literature. I. Lackey, Mercedes. II. Wilson, Leah.
     PR6068.O93Z7635 2006
     823'.914—dc22

                                                                    2005030953

Proofreading by Jessica Keet and Stacia Seaman
Cover design by Mondolithic
Text design and composition by John Reinhardt Book Design
Printed by Victor Graphics, Inc.

Distributed by Independent Publishers Group
To order call (800) 888-4741
www.ipgbook.com

For media inquiries and special sales contact Yara Abuata at yara@benbellabooks.com

Contents

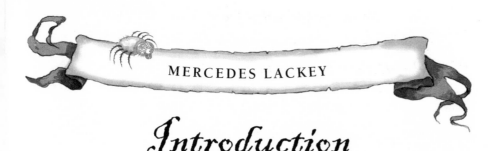

Introduction

Here are some interesting statistics to ponder:

In 2003, *Harry Potter and the Order of the Phoenix*, by J. K. Rowling, was released. According to the *Wall Street Journal*:

- 630 Barnes & Noble stores sold 286,000 copies in the first hour; 896,000 copies the first day.
- 1,200 Borders and Waldenbooks stores sold 750,000 copies in the first 23 hours, the highest first-day sales in their history.
- In the UK, WHSmith sold 120,000 copies the first day. 31,500 postmen were needed to deliver the book in England.
- In total, 5 million copies were sold the first day, shattering all records.

According to *Publishers Weekly*:

- 9.3 million copies were in print the initial week.
- 750,000 audio books were in print the initial week.
- Amazon.com, selling the $29.99 book for $12.00, shipped 789,000 copies on the first day.

The books have been published in fifty-five languages and distributed in more than 200 countries. Total copies sold for the first four Harry Potter titles, according to the *Wall Street Journal*'s January 2003 report?

- *Harry Potter and the Sorcerer's Stone*: 25.1 million
- *Harry Potter and the Chamber of Secrets*: 22 million
- *Harry Potter and the Prisoner of Azkaban*: 16.7 million
- *Harry Potter and the Goblet of Fire*: 16.3 million

The Harry Potter books are arguably the most popular in the history of modern publishing. I can think of no other books ostensibly written for children where there has been a separate set of editions with sober black-and-white covers issued so that adults could read them in public without embarrassment. I can think of no other fantasy books, even those written for adults, where one could find an entire university soccer team in line to purchase them on the first day of issue, something I saw with my own eyes when I was in the U.K.

Such success attracts a great deal of attention, not all of it positive. It has introduced a veritable horde of new would-be writers and eager readers to the hitherto murky and marginal world of fan fiction. It has engendered acrimony bordering on hysteria from those who see the books as dangerous. It has spawned an entire industry of forgers, frauds and copycats.

And it has attracted critics, both favorable and unfavorable.

This book of essays has a fair sampling of that criticism, much of it far weightier than I had originally envisioned when I agreed to be the editor of this volume. I can't say, in retrospect, that I disagree with the relative sobriety of the topics. When a set of books seems to speak so strongly to Everyman, it's a good idea to try and understand why, and what the implications are.

And that is what our diverse crop of writers has done.

A few of us have taken a humorous look at the phenomenon, while others have approached the subject in the spirit of sober critique. But all of us, I suspect, have approached the books with respect, enjoyment and, yes, even love.

Just as in the books themselves, there is something for almost everyone here. Just as in the books themselves, you'll find things to make you smile, things to make you laugh and things to make you think.

And really, that is all anyone can ask of any book.

Now, my personal reactions to the Harry Potter phenomenon.

A hundred thousand blessings on J. K. Rowling.

I'm serious here.

How many youngsters have been turned on to reading for the first time by these books? Certainly it numbers in the thousands, maybe the hundreds of thousands. For that and that alone, she should live a thousand years, all of them healthy, wealthy and happy. At a point in time where kids are getting repetitive stress problems from mousing and joysticking, to discover that the increasingly weighty books are giving kids neck strain from reading in bed—it's astonishing and, if you ask me, rather wonderful.

Then there's the fact that youngsters and adults can both read and enjoy and—do you think?—talk about the series together.

And as if that wasn't enough, Rowling addresses some serious issues in these books without getting preachy about it. She does that most dangerous of things: she gets youngsters thinking, and thinking for themselves. In her fantasy world, everything is not rainbows and puppies, cleaned-up-and-sanitized-for-your-protection. The wizarding world is dark and dangerous, and not only can you die, you may find that the people you trust are not worthy of it, the people who seem strong may be all bluff and the people you depend on may not be able to protect you. Scary stuff. Strong stuff.

And there is yet more meat in these books. All manner of issues are addressed: prejudice, intolerance, authoritarianism, exploitation and, as one author in this book points out, fascism—and all in such a way as to alarm the prejudiced, the intolerant, the authoritarian, the exploiters, the fascists. It's entertaining, without, as Heinlein said, "selling your birthright for a pot of message," guaranteeing that it will be read, and reread.

Oh, yes. The narrow-minded, and those who would like to "educate" children into submission, have a lot to fear from Harry Potter. Those who would like to feed those same children pastel-colored, sugar-coated, fluffy nothingness have just as much to fear. I hope they are shaking in their shoes. With luck, the kids who grow up reading these books will not settle for "Because I am the boss," "Because this book says so," "Because that's the way it is." With luck, they will march out there determined to figure out what is wrong and right, and to right the wrongs.

Am I, as a professional in this field, jealous of Rowling's success?

Well, no. Envious, yes—I would rather like to have a small slice of that particular pie—but I would not want to see any of her success diminished. She has earned every pound and dollar and yen and peso. I wish I could determine just what it is that she has done that has so captured the imaginations of children and adults, and apply it to my own work, not just because I would like the success, but because I think my work would be better for it.

This is not to say that I think the books are flawless, but the things they, and Rowling, have to say are more than enough to overcome the flaws.

I love these books. I reread them over and over.

Will they become classics, in the sense of Dickens, Jack London, Twain?

I don't know. I hope so. Because these books are about that, too. Hope. And there's not nearly enough of that to go around.

4

Mapping the World of Harry Potter

DANIEL P. MOLONEY

Harry Potter and the Young Man's Mistake

The Illusion of Innocence and the Temptation of Power

PASSIONS AND ILLUSIONS ARE BOTH DANGEROUS AND SEDUCTIVE. BOTH LEAD TO ERRORS IN JUDGMENT, AS DANIEL P. MOLONEY REMINDS US IN THIS ESSAY. BOTH CAN BE VALUABLE TOOLS, BOTH CAN BECOME TRAPS. AND YET, HOW DULL THE WORLD WOULD BE, EITHER THE REAL OR FICTIONAL WORLD, WITHOUT THEM!

I'VE JUST FINISHED *Harry Potter and the Half-Blood Prince*, and I'm worried about Harry. I'm still young enough to enjoy J. K. Rowling's novels as told from their adolescent hero's point of view, but I'm also old enough to be able to see beyond that point of view, and my older self is rather worried. I'm not sure it's a good idea for Harry not to return to Hogwarts for his last year; the decision seems more rash than prudent. I'm also worried that he tried to use the Cruciatus Curse on Severus Snape, as he already had tried to use it on Bellatrix Lestrange in the last pages of *Harry Potter and the Order of the Phoenix*. It seems that these curses are Unforgivable in part because they require true malice to be used effectively—at least, that's what both Lestrange and Snape tell Harry after he tries to torture them. If that's the case, then these curses require a terrible cruelty of heart, and I'm afraid that Harry's passionate

7

nature might lead him to become cruel enough to use them. I'm also worried that Harry broke up with Ginny Weasley. There's something noble and selfless about Harry's desire to face Lord Voldemort alone so that nobody else will get hurt. But there's also something dangerous about it, because it exacerbates a weakness in Harry's character—his young man's desire to be self-sufficient.

I'm older than Harry, but not as old as Albus Dumbledore, and so I am interested almost as much in Dumbledore's reflections on aging as I am in Harry's display of the virtues and defects of youth. And so while I worry about Harry, I also worry that, when I worry about him, I might be making what Dumbledore calls an "old man's mistake." I take this phrase from the end of *Order of the Phoenix*:

> "Harry, I owe you an explanation," said Dumbledore. "An explanation of an old man's mistakes. For I see now that what I have done, and not done, with regard to you, bears all the hallmarks of the failings of age. Youth cannot know how age thinks and feels. But old men are guilty if they forget what it was to be young...and I seem to have forgotten...lately."

An "old man's mistake," we subsequently discover, is to try to protect those we love from painful truths and burdensome responsibilities. Dumbledore mentions two of his own such mistakes: he tried to distance himself from Harry in order to protect him from Lord Voldemort, and he refused to tell him about the prophecy concerning him because, as he puts it, "I cared more for your happiness than your knowing the truth."

These mistakes are quite significant, for if Dumbledore hadn't made them, Harry would never have tried to enter the Ministry of Magic, and Sirius Black would not have died trying to save him. If Dumbledore had confided in Harry and trained him in Occlumency himself, Harry might have been able to defend himself from Voldemort's attempts at possession, and he certainly wouldn't have been tricked and trapped the way he was. In the fight against Voldemort, it is necessary for Harry Potter to face certain hard realities about the world and his important responsibilities within it. But Dumbledore loved Harry's innocence too much, and wants to protect that innocence by shielding him from knowledge that would force him to grow up too fast. Dumbledore loved Harry's childhood innocence too much, and this seemingly minor, otherwise forgivable fault ended up endangering the lives of several people, and costing the life of a loyal friend. Throughout the book, Harry is infected with what seems to be merely an adolescent's anger at not being treated as an adult. But in what I found to be a surprising turn of events, Harry's judgment about his own maturity and responsibility is shown to be more right than the usually impeccable Dumbledore's. Loving too much, and in the wrong way, we learn, is actually a mistake—a vice, even.

I'm trying to sort out my emotions. On the one hand, I want to protect Harry from the dangers that I see lying ahead, dangers that are as much moral as mortal. Yet I don't want to impede Harry's growth by making an old man's mistake. In this, as in many things, I think that I can learn from Dumbledore. And I can also learn from Rowling, whose tremendous success is due in no small part to her unusually keen insight into the personalities and lives of young adults. Her young heroes are believable because she really does understand kids at those ages—even to the point of making fine distinctions between thirteen-year-olds and fourteen-year-olds. And I think that she puts her finger on an aspect of contemporary child-rearing that needs to be reexamined: that adults value the innocence of children more than children do. I also think that she's right to suggest that sometimes, perhaps even most of the time, it is the children who are right and the adults who are wrong.

The Old Man's Mistake

Adults value innocence in children because they think that innocence is a rare commodity in the adult world. The love of children seems to be pure and full of joy, while the responsibilities of adulthood are full of compromises and muddling through. Children play; adults work. Children have not a care in the world; adults have to worry about children and the world. Children are, in other words, insulated from all that makes being an adult so difficult. So it is no wonder that world-weary adults see the innocence of children as something extremely valuable and worth protecting.

Rowling's books remind us that children hate it when adults think this way—when, in order to protect their "innocence," we thwart their explorations and inquiries into the adult world. Children are not under any illusion that their lives are filled with innocence. Kids can be cruel and petty, foul-mouthed and proud, merciless judges and vicious gossipers. They have jealousies and hatreds, cliques and quasi-tribal allegiances that form easily and disband just as easily. From the beginning of their time at Hogwarts, for example, Harry and Draco Malfoy are rivals, and this at first rather shallow dislike only intensifies as they get older—to the point that when Harry is groping for a spell to use against Draco, he uses the one the Half-Blood Prince had designated as "for enemies."

Children also know that their worst enemies are often themselves. Part of growing up is acquiring the self-control and the moderation that marks virtue, but often children don't control themselves even when they know that they should. In *Order of the Phoenix*, Harry takes a swing at Draco after their Quidditch match, and is punished harshly. Harry feels anger at the injustice—Draco deliberately provoked him—but he also knows that his lack of self-control betrayed him. The joy of Draco's bloody nose was fleeting compared with the punishment of being banned from Quidditch for life. Harry should have known better, but his anger was too strong, and he failed both his friends and himself. The same goes for his failure to practice his Occlumency lessons, and his procrastination during the second task in the Triwizard Tournament. On numerous occasions, Harry kicks himself for not working at something important as hard as he should, out of simple immaturity.

Children see adulthood as something desirable. They want to be given responsibility, and not just the responsibilities (such as taking out the trash) that the adults don't want. In *Order of the Phoenix*, Harry is outraged that all the adults are keeping secrets from him, especially after he has proven himself to be brave and clever and able to handle situations that would overwhelm most adults.

Rowling is of course depicting what adults will recognize as a certain sort of teenage moodiness, but in her characteristically balanced way she is also sensitive to the *reasons* for Harry's anger. Yes, he's a bundle of hormones raging out of control, but he's also the central figure in the fight against Voldemort, and he's right to think that he should be treated as such. Sometimes he's angry for no real reason, but sometimes he's angry at what he thinks is the unjust way he's being treated—and Rowling takes her teenagers seriously enough to acknowledge that they often have a point.

Children know that they lack virtue and that their lives are filled with sin and vice. That's why they want to grow up. Why, then, do adults try to protect them from adulthood?

There are all sorts of practical reasons we do this. As Rowling makes clear, we often grow up through taking on important responsibilities. We are forced to push our talents to the limits, face our own inadequacies and limitations, juggle different priorities and learn from our mistakes. When he founds Dumbledore's Army and starts training his classmates, Harry finds that he is good at teaching, and that the other students appreciate being trained to fight their recently risen enemy. For the first time, Harry finds joy not in sports or in juvenile hijinks, but in taking on an important adult responsibility and discharging it well. Likewise, when Draco is given the duty of finding a way to smuggle Death Eaters into Hogwarts, he becomes a much more serious person than before—in previous years, his purpose in life seemed limited to confirming in his own mind that he was superior to Harry. Even Percy Weasley finds tremendous satisfaction in adult responsibilities—being Head Boy and then working in the Ministry.

We've all had this experience of performing an important duty well. It typically is one of the most important and memorable moments for us, a rite of passage into maturity, when we first appreciate the intrinsic satisfaction—and fun—of fulfilling a difficult and important task. Adults often look to such moments as giving meaning to their work and to their lives. But, we tell ourselves, there are many responsibilities that are too important to entrust to teenagers. Often, it's because the tasks are complicated and difficult, and since we

11

don't want to take the time to explain them fully, we prefer to have someone more experienced take them on. That's a practical reason for "protecting" kids from the responsibilities of adulthood.

But there is also a culture-wide belief that childhood is a time of innocence that needs to be preserved and prolonged, and that to face the burdens of adulthood prematurely is a cause for sadness. I think that Rowling is right to challenge this view.

Sometimes we think this way because we aren't mature ourselves, or at least, we regard adulthood as something onerous. There's a side to Arthur Weasley that, rather than discipline Fred and George, would prefer to laugh at their antics. Ludo Bagman seems to wish that he'd never grown up, and Sirius Black feels nostalgia for his own schoolboy days. If adulthood is all joyless responsibility and burdens, then it follows that children should be protected from it as long as possible.

On the other hand, sometimes adults don't see children as real people in their own right. Children are thought to be extensions of their parents, as several people take Harry to be an extension of James and Lily or as Amos Diggory seems to regard Cedric, or as Vernon and Petunia Dursley regard Dudley. Molly Weasley, whom Rowling depicts with enormous affection, seems nonetheless to be incapable of treating her remarkable children with any sense of perspective. She seems to think adulthood and childhood don't exist on a continuum, but are entirely separate worlds that should be kept apart until the children reach the legal age of maturity. And even then, she doesn't really believe her children are adults: It's amusing that she thinks that Bill and Fleur are too young to marry, when she and Arthur actually *eloped* at a similar age.

Maturity doesn't come simply with time and experience; it comes from reflecting on experiences and learning from them. Children form their personalities with every decision they make and every lesson they learn. They aren't simply born with the personalities of little adults, or magically acquire an adult personality on their eighteenth birthday (or seventeenth, in the wizarding world). And because of this, it is a mistake to forget that they need to be challenged, trusted and given real responsibility. When we look at children we have to always keep in mind that they are works in progress and remind ourselves that they are the most important works entrusted to us.

There's a third sort of misjudgment we can make about young people: we forget that they are still young. Because we live among other adults, we grow used to their stability of character. Once we get to know an adult, we can safely assume that we won't have to revise our estimation of him or her much. But we can't make that assumption about the young, because they change rapidly. They aren't set in their ways, and can acquire new habits and outlooks quite suddenly. If we aren't paying close attention, we can lazily assume that the young man before us is the same irresponsible young boy he was a few months ago. And before we know it, he's angry at us for treating him like someone he no longer is.

So I've been trying to understand the old man's mistake, and I think I disagree with Dumbledore. He says the mistake is made by "fools in love" who love the young too much. Instead, I think, it is the mistake of not loving *them* at all. Instead of loving the teenager with all the complexities of his or her own still-forming personality, we are infatuated with the idea of "youth," or with the father in the son or with our memories of our own teenage years, or we assume we know the person we imagine is still there. We fail to love young people as the individuals they are and are becoming, and in the process fail to treat them correctly.

13

What Youth Cannot Know

If I am to avoid the old man's mistake, I have to be very careful to take the measure of Harry correctly, to see him as he actually is right now. But even taking the appropriate care, I still worry that Harry is making some mistakes, ones that seem characteristic of the immature young man.

From the vantage of his many years, and from his decades spent at Hogwarts, Dumbledore knows the defects typical of youth. The first of these is the most obvious: The young cannot know how time affects people. Of course, older people are less energetic; they find practical jokes less amusing; they tend to have set ways of doing things and are reluctant to change them. But it's a truth of simple logic that no young person can know what it is like to be older or to have seen more things happen than he or she has seen. No young person can know what it is like to grow up. On the other hand, older people have seen their classmates change and mature, and know, for example, that a person sometimes changes the ideas and beliefs he or she had as an adolescent. Young people can gain some sense of this through the reminiscence of older people, as we see starting in *Harry Potter and the Prisoner of Azkaban* when Harry meets James Potter's boyhood friend Remus Lupin and learns that his father was a high school prankster. But it is a lesson that is hard to accept until you've seen it with your own eyes.

Time is one mystery to the young. In the Department of Mysteries in the Ministry of Magic, researchers study two other mysteries so great that their secrets have yet to be cracked. Nearly Headless Nick tells Harry about one of them:

14

"I know nothing of the secrets of death, Harry, for I chose my feeble imitation of life instead. I believe learned wizards study the matter in the Department of Mysteries...."

And Dumbledore tells him about the other:

"There is a room in the Department of Mysteries," interrupted Dumbledore, "that is kept locked at all times. It contains a force that is at once more wonderful and more terrible than death, than human intelligence, than forces of nature. It is also, perhaps, the most mysterious of the many subjects for study that reside there. It is the power held within that room that you possess in such quantities and which Voldemort has not at all. That power took you to save Sirius tonight. That power also saved you from possession by Voldemort, because he could not bear to reside in a body so full of the force he detests. In the end, it mattered not that you could not close your mind. It was your heart that saved you."

Death and love are great mysteries, in part because before them we must all be humble. The first is utterly inscrutable to the living, while the second can be known only by those who surrender to it. Both are mysterious, because neither can be made susceptible to human control, although in the pride of their youth some may try. Indeed, it is here that I worry most about Harry.

The two great mysteries, death and love, are always linked. Death is always a possibility for those we love; loss is part of the risk we take in loving. Love binds us to another person; death rips our beloved from us. Normally, however, we have a long time until death parts us from our beloved. Not Harry. Harry never loved passionately while living with the Dursleys, but at Hogwarts he has made friends, learned about his parents, discovered his godfather and felt important and loved. Then, starting at the moment of his triumph in the Triwizard Tournament, his newly expanded heart starts to hurt: Cedric is killed at his side, and Lord Voldemort returns. Hogwarts is taken over by Dolores Umbridge, and Sirius is killed. Dumbledore takes Harry into his confidence, strengthening the bonds of affection between them as they plot the demise of Voldemort, and then is killed, unexpectedly, before Harry's eyes.

At the end of *Order of the Phoenix*, Harry is so numb from the loss of Sirius that he wants to bring him back from the dead. At the end of *Half-Blood Prince*, Harry's pain tempts him to stop loving altogether:

> And Harry saw very clearly as he sat there under the hot sun how people who cared about him had stood in front of him one by one, his mother, his father, his godfather, and finally Dumbledore, all determined to protect him; but now that was over. He could not let anybody else stand between him and Voldemort; he must abandon forever the illusion that he ought to have lost at the age of one, that the shelter of a parent's arms meant that nothing could hurt him....The last and greatest of his protectors had died, and he was more alone than he had ever been before.

Harry means to face Voldemort alone, without Ron and Hermione or his other friends. He breaks up with Ginny, and decides to leave

15

Hogwarts, the only place he has ever felt at home. Why does he want to cut himself off from those dearest to him? Because of the young man's mistake.

In *Harry Potter and the Sorcerer's Stone*, Dumbledore tells Harry, "To the well-organized mind, death is but the next great adventure." To one who looks at it that way, death is not something traumatic. Dumbledore acknowledges that this must seem incredible to one as young as Harry, but we are left to assume that it is one of the things we learn when we grow up. Sirius makes this point to the Weasley twins after their father is attacked by Voldemort's giant snake in *Order of the Phoenix*: "This is why you're not in the Order—you don't understand—there are things worth dying for!" Dumbledore tells the same thing to Voldemort later in *Order of the Phoenix*:

> "There is nothing worse than death, Dumbledore!" snarled Voldemort.
>
> "You are quite wrong," said Dumbledore....

16

Harry is too young to believe this. Although he doesn't worry about his own death, he is afraid to lose those he loves.

Indeed, Harry's understanding of death is not so different from Voldemort's. To both, death is sheer negation, the loss of those you love. Death deprived Tom Riddle of his mother, and threatens to deprive him of his own life (probably the only thing he truly loves). Harry also sees death as a threat to all he loves. While a mature love, according to Dumbledore, is able to accept personal loss as the beloved's gain, when Harry loses loved ones, he focuses on how they gave him comfort, companionship and protection— all the things he lacked growing up. In practice Harry doesn't see death as Dumbledore's "great adventure"; rather, his love tends to be possessive and self-referential. That's why he is so certain that Sirius would choose to be a ghost and remain with him.

Harry concludes that his love for others will only weaken him and allow others to control him. This is the same way Voldemort views love—as an encumbrance. Harry does not possess Voldemort's lust for domination, but he needs to be strong enough to overcome

Voldemort and he believes that, to be strong enough, he has to be alone. I am not so sure that Harry is right about this. In fact, I'm sure that, if Dumbledore is right, then Harry is dangerously wrong, both about love and about death. For, as Dumbledore has told him on several occasions, the only way he can defeat Lord Voldemort is through love.

An Education in Love

In *Half-Blood Prince,* Dumbledore tells Harry that only a wizard with "uncommon skill and power" can defeat Voldemort:

> "But I haven't got uncommon skill and power," said Harry, before he could stop himself.
>
> "Yes, you have," said Dumbledore firmly. "You have a power that Voldemort has never had. You can—"
>
> "I know!" said Harry impatiently. "I can love!" It was only with difficulty that he stopped himself adding, "Big deal!"
>
> "Yes, Harry, you can love," said Dumbledore.... "Which, given everything that has happened to you, is a great and remarkable thing. You are still too young to understand how unusual you are, Harry."

Harry is too young to appreciate the power of his ability to love. But Dumbledore is convinced that Harry's heart is the key to everything—so much so that, when he decides to train Harry himself, he does not teach him what one would expect (Hermione guesses that he'll teach Harry "really advanced magic, probably... powerful countercurses... anti-jinxes... and evasive enchantments generally"). Instead, Dumbledore is more interested in teaching Harry three lessons about the heart.

The first lesson is a negative lesson, about what happened to Voldemort's character because he did not learn to love. Dumbledore seems to be the only person who calls Voldemort by his real name—he even calls him "Tom" during their fight in *Order of the Phoenix*—and this reflects his knowledge that there is still a little boy behind the horrible mask. It is part of Dumbledore's great wisdom to regard Voldemort not as the terrible Lord that others perceive, but as simply a more powerful version of the young Tom Riddle: the orphan who is afraid to die, the secretive boy who doesn't want to have friends, the proud wizard who believes nothing is beyond his power. When Dumbledore shows Harry the memory of his first meeting with Tom Riddle, he calls attention to several vices that the adult Voldemort retains. The boy Tom Riddle doesn't want Dumbledore's help to go to Diagon Alley. While most children who depend on adults for everything have a desire to be self-sufficient, Dumbledore notes that the adult Riddle is still motivated by this childish desire. Likewise, the adult Voldemort still hates his father for giving him his ordinary Muggle name, and wants notoriety, just as children long to be different from others and to stand out. Children, who are weak and ignorant compared to adults, often dream of being more powerful than their peers; the adult Voldemort, just like the boy Riddle, loves to use his powers to attract and control others.

18

At bottom, then, Dumbledore sees Voldemort as the adult version of a loveless and lonely boy. This keeps him from regarding Voldemort as simply a monster. He calls Voldemort evil, a tyrant, less than human and, most accurately, "a mortal man with a maimed and diminished soul." He is not so naïve that he thinks Voldemort will ever undergo a conversion and use his powers in the service of humanity. But he also never forgets that Voldemort once was the self-possessed eleven-year-old boy who impressed him at the orphanage. Dumbledore's insight is that while Tom Riddle grew in power and knowledge, he did not grow in maturity. To become mature is to become humble, to learn to trust and depend on others, and to love. Voldemort's vices—and thus his weaknesses—are the untempered vices of his youth. They are rooted in pride, which Augustine defined as the love of self to the exclusion of others. This is the first lesson that Dumbledore tries to teach Harry.

Dumbledore also never forgets that Harry is another lonely and wounded orphan, with many of the same vices as the young Riddle. He does not have the same instincts for cruelty and domination as Riddle. But he, too, is proud; he, too, is competitive and wants to be better than others (think of his rivalry with Draco Malfoy or his dreams of winning the Triwizard Tournament). He holds grudges, and doesn't trust those who are not loyal to him (e.g., Snape). He gets into fights frequently, and has little love for his Muggle relatives. Harry is vaguely aware of his similarities with Voldemort, but Dumbledore is acutely aware of them. He seems to worry that Harry's pride might lead him to be tempted by the Dark Arts.

I think this accounts for the second lesson Dumbledore tries to teach Harry in their sessions together: that trust requires abandoning oneself to others. After being so distant from Harry in *Order of the Phoenix*, Dumbledore opens his heart to Harry, revealing how fond of him he really is, and how proud. I was especially taken by how he revealed his self-doubt and weakness to Harry; at one point during his confession of his old man's mistake, he "closed his eyes and buried his face in his long-fingered hands...[in an] uncharacteristic sign of exhaustion, or sadness." Dumbledore is a humble man to demonstrate such weakness before an angry teenager. (Phineas Nigellus, for instance, would do no such thing.) In revealing himself so, and in asking for forgiveness, he hopes to win back Harry's trust. Harry has already proclaimed his loyalty to Dumbledore, particularly as the head of "Dumbledore's Army." Later, before Rufus Scrimgeour at the Weasleys', he again professes his loyalty—agreeing that he's "Dumbledore's man through and through."

19

But immediately after telling this story to Dumbledore, and provoking the headmaster's tears, he and Dumbledore get into an argument about the nature of trust. Harry cannot believe that Dumbledore trusts Snape, and Dumbledore is sharp with Harry for refusing to trust his judgment. The argument is not resolved. Later, when Harry learns that Dumbledore also gave the young Tom Riddle the benefit of the doubt in his first years at Hogwarts, Harry thinks to himself, "Here, again, was Dumbledore's tendency to trust people in spite of overwhelming evidence that they did not deserve it!" Clearly, Harry's loyalty to Dumbledore does not lead him to trust Dumbledore's judgment about people. He cannot see any reason to trust Snape, and so he doesn't trust Dumbledore in matters concerning Snape. This disagreement is significant, because it reflects Harry's pride, his prefer-ence for his own judgment about Snape despite the assurances of Dumbledore. All the members of the Order of the Phoenix, even Sirius, trust Snape because Dumbledore does, yet Harry cannot.

Dumbledore sees this as a key moment in Harry's formation. Dumbledore is known, and often loved, for his willingness to trust others, to forgive them, to show them mercy, to let them have second chances when others won't. The importance of trust seems to be a central conviction of his, and he wants to teach it to Harry. So he gives him an assignment. He calls it "a grave responsibility," and tries to impress on Harry its importance, but he refuses to explain why. I'm referring, of course, to the task of persuading Horace Slughorn to hand over the memory of his conversations with the young Tom Riddle. Harry's not the only one who doesn't understand what Dumbledore is up to:

20

> As he closed the study door behind him, [Harry] distinctly heard Phineas Nigellus say, "I can't see why the boy should be able to do it better than you, Dumbledore."
>
> "I wouldn't expect you to, Phineas," replied Dumbledore, and Fawkes gave another low, musical cry.

We know what happens: Harry makes a couple of feeble attempts to talk to Slughorn, but when he doesn't meet with quick success, he gets distracted and eventually loses interest. At his next meeting with Dumbledore he realizes that he had not put much effort into this task, and feels embarrassed and ashamed. Dumbledore doesn't accept any of his excuses, nor does he spare Harry's feelings. Rather, he makes his disappointment clear to Harry, and then waits in silence for an apology. Eventually, Harry blurts out, "I should have realized you wouldn't have asked me to do it if it wasn't really important. . . . I'll get it from him." This satisfies Dumbledore, and they move on.

It's clearly an important scene. But what's going on here? I think that Dumbledore is trying to teach Harry to trust, even when he doesn't understand why. Dumbledore could easily have framed this assignment differently. He might have explained Horcruxes, for instance, or suggested that Slughorn's memory would reveal how to kill Lord Voldemort. Had he done so, Harry would have seen the point of his assignment and been motivated to try harder; he would have made the task his own. But Dumbledore doesn't just want the memory—that's where Phineas is mistaken. He wants Harry's trust. He wants Harry to want the memory just because Dumbledore has asked him to get it. He wants Harry to trust his judgment that this is a very important task, even if he doesn't understand why. To Dumbledore, real loyalty requires deeds, not just words.

A few pages later, we realize that Harry is not the first student to whom Dumbledore has tried to teach this lesson. In the Pensieve, we witness a scene from Dumbledore's office from decades before, in which Voldemort sat where Harry sits, and, like Harry, Voldemort expresses skepticism about the importance Dumbledore gives to love. Dumbledore tries, gently but firmly, to provoke Voldemort to examine his conscience, to consider the evil he has done. Dumbledore fails, of course.

21

> For the first time, Voldemort smiled.... "The old argument," he said softly. "But *nothing I have seen in the world* has supported your famous pronouncements that love is more powerful than my kind of magic, Dumbledore." [emphasis added]

Voldemort trusts his own judgment, not Dumbledore's greater experience. Their difference of opinion over love leads them to conclude that they have nothing more to say to each other. Voldemort is filled with rage at being thwarted, but Dumbledore has a different reaction to their final parting of ways: "a great sadness filled his face." Dumbledore has lost the heart of his student for good, and he wishes things were different. It seems that he still loves Tom Riddle, even though they are explicitly enemies.

Harry witnesses this scene, but he doesn't seem to realize the parallels between Voldemort's encounter with Dumbledore and his own. Nothing that Harry has seen has supported Dumbledore's famous pronouncements either. So there's only one way Dumbledore can prepare Harry to give enough importance to love—he has to teach him to believe in what he has not experienced himself. He has to trust Dumbledore, blindly. This is the second lesson. I'm worried that Harry doesn't get it.

Dumbledore tries to teach Harry a third lesson in their meetings together, a lesson about the importance of friendship. In the Weasleys' spider-filled broomstick shed, he urges Harry to tell everything about Trelawney's prophecy to Hermione and Ron. Harry is startled at this suggestion, but Dumbledore insists. "You do them a disservice by not confiding something this important to them. . . . You need your friends, Harry," he warns. Harry's instinct is to keep this prophecy to himself. Dumbledore ventures two reasons why:

> "I didn't want—"
>
> "—to worry or frighten them?" said Dumbledore, surveying Harry over the top of his half-moon spectacles. "Or perhaps to confess that you yourself are worried and frightened?"

22 Dumbledore is probably right on both counts.

This is the second time Harry has isolated himself out of a dramatic sense of self-sacrifice, and the second time Dumbledore has had to stop him. In *Order of the Phoenix*, Harry resolves to return to the Dursleys' house because he thinks he is being possessed by Voldemort and that to "cut himself off from other wizards entirely" is the only way to protect his friends. Or at least, that's his ostensible reason. As Phineas Nigellus recognizes, however, Harry also seems to take pleasure in feeling sorry for himself; he even feels "a savage pleasure that he was giving the others the opportunity to keep talking about him, as they were bound to be doing." Phineas' speech to Harry is right on the money:

> "This is precisely why I *loathed* being a teacher. Young people are so infernally convinced that they are absolutely right about everything. Has it not occurred to you, my poor puffed-up popinjay, that there might be an excellent reason why the headmaster of Hogwarts is not confiding every detail of his plans to you? Have you never paused, while feeling hard-done-by, to note that following Dumbledore's orders has never yet led you into harm? No. No, like all young people,

you are quite sure that you alone feel and think, you alone recognize danger, you alone are the only one clever enough to realize what the Dark Lord might be planning...."

Sirius describes Phineas as the "least popular headmaster Hogwarts ever had," and here we can see why. Yet I don't think Dumbledore would disagree with his assessment of young men in general and, at this moment, of Harry in particular. Harry is wallowing in self-pity, and it takes his friends to rescue him. Our friends bring us out of ourselves. They can often provide perspective when we are sad or, if nothing else, support. After this scene, for instance, Ginny brings Harry out of his self-pity by reminding him that she actually has been possessed by Voldemort (in *Harry Potter and the Chamber of Secrets*) and her experience was nothing like his. Harry is brought up short by this, both because Ginny makes a good point, and because he had forgotten that Ginny and he were linked in this way.

Dumbledore knows that having friends is often the best way to insure against self-love. Self-absorbed people don't have friends but rather admirers, cronies, servants, allies or something else: Gilderoy Lockhart, despite his legions of fans, doesn't have a single person with whom he can be honest. Slughorn doesn't have any friends, but rather former students whom he collects. Draco doesn't really have friends, it seems—that's why he's crying to Moaning Myrtle in the bathroom. Nor, as Dumbledore frequently mentions, does Tom Riddle have (or want) any friends. Harry grew up without friends, and knows that he can survive on his own. This gives him the strength to do unpopular things that he thinks are right. But Harry's background also tricks him into thinking that he doesn't need the companionship of people he loves. This is yet another young person's mistake.

Imagine if Harry actually does try to face Voldemort without Ron, Hermione, the Weasleys, the Order of the Phoenix or any of the rest of his friends and allies at Hogwarts. He might begin with noble ideals, but his mission is one of vengeance, and he is looking for those he hates. Wouldn't it be tempting for him to dip into the Dark Arts, looking for weapons that could help him kill Voldemort? How useful are his skills at *defense* against the Dark Arts for his goal of *attacking* his enemies? He needs curses, not countercurses. He has already tried to use the Cruciatus Curse on Bellatrix Lestrange and on Snape, and the *Sectumsempra* on Draco. What's to keep him from going further? The Sorting Hat saw that he would make a great Slytherin, which means he probably has the talent for the Dark Arts. Yes, Harry would have to cultivate his hatred, because you can't curse somebody without malice, but why shouldn't he feel malice toward Snape, Bellatrix, Wormtail, the Malfoys, and the rest of the Death Eaters, not to mention Voldemort? It would be very easy for Harry to become a rather accomplished practitioner of the Dark Arts, I would think, were he not around those who love him. Dumbledore even so much as tells him this:

> "Harry, despite your privileged insight into Voldemort's world...you have never been seduced by the Dark Arts, never, even for a second, shown the slightest desire to become one of Voldemort's followers!... You are protected, in short, by your ability to love!" said Dumbledore loudly. "The only protection that can possibly work against the lure of power like Voldemort's!"

If we turn Dumbledore's last statement around, we can see that were Harry to stop loving, he would lose his protection against the allure of the Dark Arts. This is what Dumbledore believes to be at stake.

There seem to be two reasons that people enter the service of Lord Voldemort: either they are bigoted against those who aren't wizards, as the Malfoys and the Lestranges are, or they desire power and control over others and gradually forget how to love. As Professor Quirrell sums up the second point of view: "Lord Voldemort showed me how wrong I was. There is no good and evil, there is only power, and those too weak to seek it...." Harry is not a bigot, but he might be persuaded that he needs more power, and this might lead him to the Dark Arts.

So this is why I am worried about Harry. If Dumbledore's philosophy is correct, then it is essential that Harry learn to trust and continue to love. Harry has been marked by love, and protected by love, and has even fallen in love. But he also has been hurt by love, and might not want to be hurt again. As he has grown, he has developed a strong tendency to trust only himself, and it seems likely that Dumbledore's lesson on the nature of trust—a lesson Harry found difficult to learn in the first place—was undone by the headmaster's death at the hands of the man he trusted. And unlike Dumbledore, who can love his enemies and forgive those who betray him, Harry does not seem open to mercy. I think there is a real risk that Harry will not listen to his mentor, and in avenging Dumbledore become everything Dumbledore warned him against: Rowling has made the parallels between Harry and Voldemort too strong for this danger not to be real.

If Harry is to keep his heart pure, he will need to be surrounded by people who won't let him withdraw into himself, and who can warn him against the mistakes typical of youth. So I'm encouraged that he will begin the summer surrounded by his adopted family at the wedding between Bill Weasley and Fleur Delacour. And I'm even more heartened that Ron and Hermione know they have to stick close to Harry, to keep him from "protecting" them by slipping off by himself. They love him, but in this matter they don't—and shouldn't—trust him.

25

I am not sure that Harry's friends will be of much practical help in the fight against Voldemort. I expect that Harry will eventually face him alone. But if we trust in Dumbledore's philosophy, then we should also trust in the power of friendship to protect Harry's heart, which we know is the real key to victory, even if Harry doesn't believe it. In which case, if I am to trust Dumbledore, then I should also trust Ron and Hermione's friendship. As long as they are worrying about Harry, I don't have to.

DANIEL P. MOLONEY has a B.A. in religious studies from Yale and a doctorate in philosophy from Notre Dame. He has taught in the Department of Philosophy at Notre Dame and the Politics Department at Princeton. A former editor at *First Things*, he has written for *First*

Things, *Wall Street Journal*, *National Review*, *Crisis* and *American Prospect*, among other publications. He is also a contributor to BenBella's Smart Pop anthology on Phillip Pullman's His Dark Materials trilogy. He now lives in Rome, preparing for his next great adventure.

The Dursleys
as Social Commentary

THE DREADFUL DURSLEYS! ROBERTA GELLIS MAKES A POWERFUL
ARGUMENT FOR THE USE OF THE DURSLEYS AS EXAMPLES OF WHAT
NOT TO BE. FROM THE GREED OF DUDLEY TO THE ARROGANCE OF
UNCLE VERNON TO THE INTOLERANCE OF AUNT PETUNIA, GELL-
IS SUGGESTS, THE DURSLEYS PROVIDE A MORALITY PLAY HUMOROUS
IN EXECUTION BUT QUITE SERIOUS IN INTENT.

As I SIT DOWN TO WRITE THIS ESSAY, I am vividly re-
minded of a delightful (and probably apocryphal)
anecdote about Jean Cocteau, the legendary producer of the 1946 classic film *Beauty and the Beast*.
Soon after its release, Cocteau was presented with
a review of the film. It was an excellent review, which found great
depth and significance in the work, and went on to detail the meaning of various scenes and dialogues. When asked what he thought of
the review, Cocteau is said to have replied (the exchange was naturally in French, not English) that he found it quite wonderful, as he
never would have thought of it himself.

It is almost certainly true that Cocteau was joking (or being sardonic) because he was a serious and thoughtful artist; nonetheless
I do wonder as I analyze this and that in the scenes in which the
Dursleys appear whether I am finding more than Rowling intended in them. She said when asked whether there is more to Dudley
than meets the eye, "No. What you see is what you get. I am hap-

py to say that he is a character without much backstory. He is just Dudley."[1]

The comment may well have applied to the purpose of Dudley in the plot of the Harry Potter books, however, not to what Dudley exposes about the author's feeling about such a character, or how the author intends the character to affect the reader. And this would seem to be the opinion of some critics of Ms. Rowling's work. For example, William Safire does not seem to believe there is any significance in the books. He says, "These are not, however, books for adults. Unlike *Huckleberry Finn* or *Alice in Wonderland*, the Potter series is not written on two levels. . . ."[2] And Stephen King (could he be a bit envious?) asks whether there is much going on in *Harry Potter and the Goblet of Fire* besides fun and answers his own question by saying "not much."[3]

28

The extremely lively discussions concerning the content of Rowling's work contradict these denials of significance. In fact, that the characters in the Harry Potter books do affect the readers is one point of agreement among both those who wish to ban the Rowling books and those who think them beneficial.[4] And those effects are a legitimate subject for examination, whether or not the effect on the reader is a deliberate or accidental result of the author's work.

Certainly there is a growing cadre of scholarly investigation of the Harry Potter books which finds—and without straining or seeking in the ether—many levels of meaning. Lana R. Whited, in the Introduction to *The Ivory Tower and Harry Potter*, states, "Rowling herself appears to be very seriously attempting a literary achievement."[5]

Roni Natov, in direct contradiction of Safire's and King's (and a

---

[1] Interview from Scholastic Online, Oct. 6, 2000.

[2] William Safire, "Besotted with Potter," the *New York Times*, Jan. 27, 2000.

[3] Stephen King, "Wild about Harry," Review of *Harry Potter and the Goblet of Fire* by J. K. Rowling in *The New York Times Book Review*, July 23, 2000, pp. 13–14.

[4] For example, among many others: "Does Harry Potter belong in schools?" Editorial Opinion, *The Atlanta Journal-Constitution*, Oct. 5, 1999. "'Muggles' seek to muzzle Harry Potter in schools," Reuters, Oct. 13, 1999. Kimbra Wilder Gish, "Hunting Down Harry Potter: An Exploration of Religious Concerns about Children's Literature," *Horn Book*, May/June 2000, pp. 262–271. *First Things* Endorses Harry Potter, Online: Harry Potter Culture and Religion, http://www.cesnur.org.

[5] Lana R. Whited, *The Ivory Tower and Harry Potter*, University of Missouri Press, Columbia, MO, 2002, p. 11.

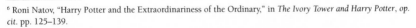

number of others') dismissal, points out that Rowling's books, unlike C.S. Lewis' or Madeline L'Engle's, or J. R. R. Tolkien's (all of which are recognized as literary achievements), "which all take place in worlds quite separate from our own, show the interpenetration of the Muggle World and that of the wizards."[6] This technique is not original— several science fiction/fantasy writers, like Emma Bull in *The War of the Oaks* and Mercedes Lackey in her SERRAted Edge series, use a real world penetrated by magic. But Rowling uses this interpenetration for social commentary on several levels.

Karen E. Westman states that "Rowling's books and their wizarding world offer not simply a fantasy of escape, but a radical way to explore very real issues in contemporary readers' lives."[7] Steven Weisman agrees, writing that "the context of the book is magic, but its subject is society."[8]

Moreover, I have found that these real issues have been addressed on at least two levels. For older readers, Rowling's attempts to educate and influence are seriously and subtly presented in situations in Hogwarts and on the greater wizarding scene. But for the younger children there are more direct attempts to teach about such things as intolerance and greed. These unpleasant characteristics are illustrated by the Dursleys in such a way that any child would wish to avoid them. And the Dursleys serve other important purposes in the Harry Potter books.

The first and most significant use of the family is to present Harry as a Cinderella archetype. He is immediately seen as the oppressed, unvalued member of a family in comfortable circumstances. Cinderella (at least in the versions I've read) sleeps in the ashes of the kitchen fire; Harry is relegated to a cupboard under the stairs. Cinderella does all the hard work; so does Harry. "While Dudley lolled around watching and eating ice cream, Harry cleaned the windows, washed the car, mowed the lawn, trimmed the flowerbeds, pruned and wa-

---

[6] Roni Natov, "Harry Potter and the Extraordinariness of the Ordinary," in *The Ivory Tower and Harry Potter, op. cit.* pp. 125–139.

[7] Karen E. Westman, "Specters of Thatcherism," in *The Ivory Tower and Harry Potter, op. cit.* p. 308.

[8] Steven Weisman, "A Novel that Is a Midsummer Night's Dream," the *New York Times*, July 11, 2000, p. A30.

tered the roses, and repainted the garden bench" (*Harry Potter and the Chamber of Secrets*). Harry's Aunt Petunia is obviously the wicked stepmother (although she does now and again exhibit qualms, which Cinderella's stepmother never does), and Dudley serves as the malignant and indulged "sisters."

Here immediately were the old friends of my childhood. Not only was I taken, as were millions of others, by the warmth and charm of the book, but half-consciously I noted that part of the pleasure I received was owing to feeling familiar and at home in these "new" surroundings. I knew when the letter arrived from Hogwarts that Harry would be refused permission to go, as Cinderella was refused permission to attend the ball even though she was included in the invitation.

Most readers would know, too, that a "fairy godmother" would intervene and make sure that Harry/Cinderella would get to the ball. That does not make Hagrid's appearance less exciting or interesting; it merely allows a reader to entertain a lively sense of anticipation instead of being depressed or frightened by Vernon Dursley's machinations. All the while Vernon tries in increasingly ridiculous ways to thwart fate, readers can foresee a happy outcome.

The Cinderella theme is the most obvious use of the Dursleys. However, especially in the early books, Vernon, Petunia and Dudley are the sources of broad, even farcical humor, with which Rowling presents social commentary and cements a young reader's distaste for anything connected with the Dursleys.

Harry's identification with Cinderella, his oppressed and hopeless existence, could have been done "straight," painted in dark colors with somber words. That technique would have served the purpose of making Harry a sympathetic figure, and connecting him with the Cinderella archetype—but it would not have won 35 million (or however many more there are by now) readers. The Harry Potter books are delightful because no matter how much our hearts ache for poor Harry's suffering, much of the time we are laughing (or, perhaps, giggling is a more accurate description) and both the aching and the laughter are owing to the Dursleys.

Rowling's presentation of Vernon, Petunia and Dudley lifts many events from the dreadful into the comical; it is pure farce. They are ridiculous and unbelievable, but not as fairy tales are unbelievable while still resonating with our deepest and most primitive instincts—the Dursleys are silly unbelievable. Take for example the scene where Vernon is nailing up the mail slot so no more letters can be delivered for Harry, which, Vernon says, will make Hogwarts stop sending letters. Petunia has doubts that the process will work. "'Oh, these people's minds work in strange ways, Petunia, they're not like you and me,' said Uncle Vernon, trying to knock in a nail with the piece of fruitcake Aunt Petunia had just brought him" (*Harry Potter and the Sorcerer's Stone*).

There might have been something dreadful and foreboding about that nailing up of the mail slot. In fact, the act does presage more and more desperate attempts to keep Harry from attending Hogwarts, but that piece of fruitcake had me grinning too broadly to worry. In fact, for me, that piece of fruitcake (fruitcakes are notoriously unyielding, but I had a most vivid image of what Aunt Petunia's were like) lifted the entire episode into comic relief.

At first, humor predominates: We have Vernon humming "Tiptoe through the Tulips" as he boards up the cracks around the doors, only to find letters rolled up inside the eggs the milkman delivered. And, of course, the letters pursue the family wherever it goes, whether that is an obscure and uncomfortable hotel or an abandoned shack on an island without any method of communication with the rest of the world.

Apparently the purpose of Vernon's futile obstinacy was to show him to be so stupid that even an eight-year-old would no longer admire his "strength" in dealing with Harry. Any child would have realized Harry could not be hidden by the third time the letters were correctly addressed, particularly to such unlikely places as "The Cupboard Under the Stairs" and "The Floor, Hut on the Rock, The Sea." But Vernon's behavior also brings a darker note into the book. In fact, by the time that Dudley asks his mother whether his father has gone mad, the wild hysteria of the attempt to escape and the desolation of the last refuge might well be frightening to children.

Hagrid's arrival lifts the cloud. Every child (and most adult readers) will be smiling over the birthday cake, the sausages and kettle to make tea, and all the other items that come out of Hagrid's pockets. What is more, readers will be settling down eagerly to learn of the Dursleys' comeuppance. And after Hagrid's rage over the Dursleys' treatment of Harry and the various instances of his successful use of magic, readers no doubt expect a serious punishment.

Dudley's pig's tail is a highly clever solution to the problem, and again puts the seal of farce on the Dursleys. There can be no doubt that Vernon or Dudley or both deserved to be turned into pigs. Both were greedy and vicious (not that pigs are customarily vicious, but they can be). But there is something truly dreadful about involuntarily losing all humanity. That Rowling is aware of this is plain from the way she writes about Professor Lupin and his life as a werewolf.

Note that Lupin is transformed into the classical werewolf, really a soulless and senseless beast, not the werewolf of fantasy literature who retains a man's mind. And Lupin himself is horrified by his temporary loss of humanity. He tells Harry, "[Parents] will not want a werewolf teaching their children, Harry. And after last night, I see their point. I could have bitten any of you.... That must never happen again" (*Harry Potter and the Prisoner of Azkaban*).

There might be as much horror and revulsion as justified satisfaction if Vernon or Dudley were turned into a pig—not to mention the complication for a careful author of the Dursleys needing magical assistance to reverse the condition. (I must admit that I wondered how the Dursleys managed to return to the mainland when Hagrid had taken their boat; it was one of the very few places in Rowling's six books where my suspension of disbelief was disturbed.)

The malfunction of Hagrid's broken wand is the perfect solution. Dudley with a pig's tail is entirely appropriate and brings the story back into farce. And there is an amusing concurrence when the Dursleys are willing to drop Harry off at King's Cross Station because they are going to London anyway to have Dudley's tail removed.

Another advantage of treating the Dursleys' unpleasant behavior as farce is to make what they do and what they are entirely repugnant, particularly to children. There can be an attraction to evil when it is strong and clever. Although a reader might be infuriated over

Snape's unfair treatment of Harry and his fellow Gryffindor house-mates, that reader could feel a sneaking admiration also.

The Dursleys, on the other hand, are ridiculous. For example, Dudley's rampant greed, as illustrated in the scene about his birthday presents, makes a reader laugh and sneer at the same time. Children are naturally greedy, but Dudley, counting his presents, is then unable to add the two his mother promises to buy to the thirty-seven he already has; Petunia must tell him he will have thirty-nine presents in total.

Rowling is careful to show that Dudley is not only greedy and stupid, but also careless and indifferent with what he receives. "Dudley had already broken his new video camera, crashed his remote control airplane, and, first time out on his racing bike, knocked down old Mrs. Figg as she crossed Privet Drive on her crutches" (*Sorcerer's Stone*). And she makes it clear that Dudley has always been this way.

When Harry is finally given a bedroom after Vernon is frightened by the letter from Hogwarts which is addressed to "The Cupboard under the Stairs," it is the room "where Dudley kept all the toys and things that wouldn't fit into his first bedroom" (*Sorcerer's Stone*). And Rowling takes the opportunity not only to point out the waste but to add to it evidence of Dudley's cruelty (the tank he had driven over a neighbor's dog), his carelessness (when he swapped a parrot for an air rifle and then carelessly bent the end by sitting on it), and his stupidity (the shelves full of books that had never been touched).

This is not because Rowling objects to consumerism as such. She is not trying to contrast an "evil" Muggle materialism with a "good" unmaterialistic wizarding world. Wizards are shown to be just as materialistic as Muggles. Indeed in that respect, as in most others, the Muggle world and the wizarding world are very similar: Diagon Alley offers different but equally alluring temptations to buy. It is the individual's way of dealing with consumerism that Rowling finds significant—not the act in itself.

Not that Harry is at first able to deal wisely with his wealth when he is made aware of his very large inheritance. Rowling is astute enough not to make Harry's resistance to buying everything in Diagon Alley the result of noble understanding on his part. It would be unbelievable for a child who never had anything at all not to grab. And Harry does.

He wants to buy a solid gold cauldron instead of the pewter one on the school list and must be restrained from the extravagance by Hagrid. He has every intention of buying a book called *Curses and Countercurses (Bewitch Your Friends and Befuddle Your Enemies with the Latest Revenges: Hair Loss, Jelly-Legs, Tongue-Tying and Much, Much More)* to use on Dudley and must be physically dragged away by Hagrid and told he is not allowed to do magic in the Muggle world.

The essential difference between Harry and Dudley—what makes Harry's consumerism acceptable and Dudley's contemptible—is what they do with their purchases. Dudley uses his to hurt people and indifferently destroys his toys. But on the train to Hogwarts, when Harry does buy far too many treats, he promptly shares them. Harry, unlike Dudley (who never offered to share even a broken toy with Harry), offers what he has to Ron as soon as he realizes Ron cannot afford to buy his own. And even two years later, Harry is sorely tempted during his two-week stay in Diagon Alley to buy a new, superior and very expensive broomstick, but by then has learned a self-control that Dudley never learns, and reminds himself that he has a perfectly good broomstick already and that his inheritance must last until he graduates from Hogwarts.

Another swipe is taken at Dudley's materialistic greed, which is made even more unpleasant by being mixed with hypocrisy, at the beginning of Aunt Marge's visit. "Harry knew perfectly well that Dudley only put up with Aunt Marge's hugs because he was well paid for it, and sure enough, when they broke apart, Dudley had a crisp twenty-pound note clenched in his fat fist" (*Prisoner of Azkaban*).

Materialism as a whole gets short shrift from Rowling. The entire segment of *Chamber of Secrets* that deals with the visit of the Masons is both funny and repulsive, with Vernon drilling his family in what they are to say and do. Rowling makes clear from the first mention that the visit is not based on any liking for the people who will be their guests but only on what profit can be made from them.

Vernon begins by saying, "This could well be the day that I make

34

the biggest deal of my career," following it with a set scenario for greeting the guests that eliminates even the smallest chance that any genuine enthusiasm for the people might be involved. We do not even learn the names of the visitors until Dudley "put on a foul, simpering smile. 'May I take your coats, Mr. and Mrs. Mason?'"

Naturally after all this preparation the reader is sure that everything will go wrong, and so it does. In a series of scenes of escalating farce, the house-elf Dobby pleads with and then tries to force Harry to promise not to return to Hogwarts. His methods increasingly disrupt the Dursleys' dinner party and the arrival of an owl with a message from the Ministry of Magic drives the Masons from the Dursleys' house, ending Vernon's hopes for a large order of drills. And the funniest thing about the entire episode is that if the Dursleys had from the beginning acknowledged Harry was a wizard, Vernon would very likely have had his order for drills.

It is interesting that Rowling spends less and less time on this kind of social commentary as the series progresses. By book six, *Harry Potter and the Half-Blood Prince,* Rowling barely mentions the Dursleys with their greed and hypocrisy. Here Rowling reserves her criticism for more powerful targets than the petty bourgeois like the Dursleys by taking aim at the head of the government.

Rowling's contempt for politicians is displayed in the inhumanity of the Prime Minister, whose concern over the disasters of the past week is concentrated on their affect on his career. Not once does the Prime Minister mention the loss of life or human tragedy caused by the collapse of a bridge or the hurricane, and his attitude toward two particularly gruesome murders is irritation over the trouble they have caused him rather than sympathy or horror. The wizarding community comes off no better; the representatives of the Ministry of Magic are even less palatable than the Muggle minister.

However, there is one issue that appears in every book in the series, and that is intolerance. Rowling begins, as usual, with the Dursleys. Vernon and Petunia are incapable of accepting that Harry is *different*, that the difference is part of him and cannot be removed. They *cannot* tolerate his difference.

This intolerance creates a darker, less humorous side to the segment about the Masons. There is something ugly and unpleasant (for all readers, I suspect, but particularly for children, who are extremely sensitive about being ignored) in the relegation of Harry to invisibility. Each member of the Dursley family has a role: Dudley is to greet the visitors at the door, and Vernon will lead them to the lounge where Petunia will wait to welcome them "graciously to our home." After detailing this, Vernon turns on Harry and says, "And *you*?" To which Harry replies, "I'll be in my bedroom, making no noise and pretending I'm not there."

At first Rowling treats the desperate attempts of the Dursleys *not to be different* with her usual humor. Vernon expresses his dislike of anyone wearing odd clothing and sputters in utter dismay when he hears some of these people mention Harry. Petunia constantly cranes her long neck to watch what her neighbors are doing.

Vernon and Petunia wish to emulate in every possible way the exact lifestyle of their neighbors on Privet Drive. Harry is, of course, different; he is of wizard blood. Vernon and Petunia are absolutely determined to squash any magic he has out of him so that he will not embarrass them before their neighbors. But strange things do happen around Harry, so until they can destroy Harry's magic they try to keep him hidden.

Any difference large or small is to be avoided, and in *Sorcerer's Stone,* the incidents Rowling chooses to make the point are funny. When Harry is being pursued by Dudley and his friends, he suddenly levitates to the roof of the school kitchens. Harry is severely punished for this because the Dursleys received an angry letter from the headmistress. He is punished again for talking to a snake in the zoo. Even in so minor and ridiculous a matter as how Harry's hair grows Vernon and Petunia want conformity. Harry's hair should lie flat, like everyone else's; when a trip to a barber does not succeed in taming his cowlick, Petunia cuts his hair so short he is nearly bald.

The passionate desire of Vernon and Petunia to be exactly the same as their bourgeois neighbors might only be another aspect of stupidity on their part and farce on Rowling's, if they applied the need for conformity only to themselves. It is because they insist that everyone else also conform that their passion to be ordinary becomes intolerance. In an interview, Rowling was asked, "If there were one thing you could change about the world, what would it be?" and her reply was, "I would make each and every one of us much more tolerant."[9]

Intolerance grows to be what I believe is the major issue in Rowling's work. It is apparently too important to be confined to criticism through the Dursleys. Intolerance is the canker at the heart of the rose of life in Hogwarts and is the one social/moral issue that Rowling treats not only through the Dursleys but with growing emphasis in Hogwarts and the wizarding world at large.

It is intolerance that nearly destroyed Hogwarts early in its history, when Salazar Slytherin wished to exclude any student who was not of pure-blood wizard ancestry. And it is this same intolerance, the basis of much of the conflict in the series, that is a consistent thread through all six books, becoming the major theme of social criticism in *Half-Blood Prince*.

Having made her points about greed and intolerance, primarily in the first three books, Rowling presents nothing new about the Dursleys in *Goblet of Fire* and *Harry Potter and the Order of the Phoenix*. Less and less space is devoted to the periods Harry spends in Privet Drive, and by *Half-Blood Prince*, the Dursleys have become totally insignificant. The only point Rowling makes in the few pages devoted to them is that Vernon and Petunia's indulgence has done a grave injury to Dudley.

Possibly this remark has some significance and there will be a satisfactory denouement concerning the Dursleys in the final volume. That, of course, remains to be seen. It may be that Rowling's comment in her interview with Scholastic Online (October 6, 2000) about there being no backstory to Dudley indicates a loss of interest in characters that have played their parts and have no future. I sincerely hope not. I cannot help but hope that there will be some closure to the relationship between Harry and his relations, although I freely admit I have no idea how Rowling will bring about that closure.

---

[9] Interview on Scholastic.com, Oct. 6, 2000.

ROBERTA GELLIS has a varied educational background—a master's degree in biochemistry and another in medieval literature—and working history: ten years as a research chemist, many years as a freelance editor of scientific manuscripts and well over thirty years as a writer. One of the most successful writers of historical fiction of the last few decades, she has published about twenty-five meticulously researched historical novels since 1964. She has been the recipient of many awards, including the Silver and Gold Medal Porgy for historical novels from *West Coast Review of Books*, the Golden Certificate and Golden Pen from Affaire de Coeur, *The Romantic Times* Award for Best Novel in the Medieval Period and Lifetime Achievement Award for Historical Fantasy, and Romance Writers of America's Lifetime Achievement Award.

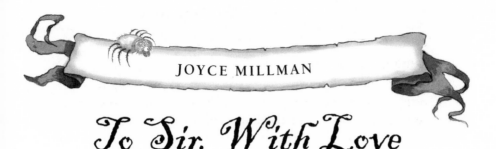

To Sir, With Love

How Fan Fiction Transformed Professor Snape from a Greasy Git to a Byronic Hero... Who's Really, Really into S/M

MOST POPULAR CULTURE HAS LONG ENGENDERED ITS OWN FLAT-
TERY-BY-IMITATION IN THE FORM OF FAN FICTION, BUT RARELY
HAS FAN FICTION DELVED INTO THE DARK AND STORMY DEPTHS
OF... ALTERNATE LIFESTYLES... AS IN THE FEVERED PRODUCTS OF
THE AFICIONADOS OF PROFESSOR SNAPE. EVEN ROWLING SEEMS
TO REALIZE THAT SHE CREATED A MONSTER... AND NOT THE ONE
SHE INTENDED.

FOR A SARCASTIC, HOOK-NOSED, greasy-haired git, Professor Severus Snape sure gets a lot of action. Down in his dungeon apartment at Hogwarts, the Potions Master has a big, curtained bed with silk sheets in Slytherin green or black (the same colors as his silk underwear). He is never lacking for sexual partners: schoolgirls, schoolboys, witches, wizards, prostitutes, colleagues, he has had them all. Snape is an expert lover, seductive and inventively sadistic. He has a secret passion for the tango. He is a stickler for old-fashioned formality. He's also a stickler for old-fashioned discipline, spanking naughty students over his knee (usually before sexually ravaging them on his desk). Severus Snape is living large but, still, he suffers—oh, how he suffers! He is hated, feared, alone. Long ago, he loved a woman. Or a man. Whatever. The point is, it ended badly. But his frozen heart has been thawed by, a) Hermione; b) Harry; c) Draco; d) All of the above. He is heterosexual, homosexual, bisexual, omnisexual, a virgin. And, oh yes—he masturbates a lot. In the shower.

Clearly, this is not your child's Severus Snape (unless your child has a precocious imagination and an Internet account). This is the Severus Snape of adult Harry Potter fan fiction, and for many (usually female) Potter fans, he is the real star of J. K. Rowling's saga. (There are plenty of PG-rated Potter fics, but for the purposes of this essay, I am concentrating on stories with ratings of R and NC-17.) This sexed-up, communal-fantasy Snape slinks through tens of thousands of fan fictions published on Web sites like *Occlumency* and *AdultFanFiction.net* and in age-restricted chat groups. The transformation of Rowling's sneering antagonist into a hunky hero is almost as fascinating as the Potter series itself, demonstrating the intense relationship between readers and fictional characters in the age of instant Internet gratification. J. K. Rowling can't publish her books fast enough, so Potterheads have hijacked her characters (all of them, not just Snape) and written their own stories, with varying degrees of skill and flair. And while Rowling has been comparatively tolerant about what other authors, such as Anne Rice, have denounced as copyright infringement, it's difficult to dispel the sense that Potter fan fiction is a runaway train bearing down on traditional publishing. After you have taken the leap and read fan fiction, is it possible to be a Potter virgin again, to be satisfied with what Rowling gives you? How has Rowling responded to fans taking possession of her characters? Who really owns Severus Snape? And how in the name of Merlin did he become the sexiest wizard alive?

The Man in Black

In an interview collected in the children's book *Conversations with J. K. Rowling*, Rowling explains that Professor Snape is loosely based on an elementary school teacher she had whose bullying of students was "the worst, shabbiest thing" an adult could do to children. In *Harry Potter and the Sorcerer's Stone*, Rowling's first descriptions of

Snape set a menacing tone: "His eyes were black...they were cold and empty and made you think of dark tunnels"; "He spoke in barely more than a whisper." In *Harry Potter and the Chamber of Secrets,* Rowling adds that the Potions Master is "cruel, sarcastic and disliked by everybody except for students from his own house," and that he gives Harry "the impression of being able to read minds." Sweeping through the corridors with "his black robes rippling in a cold breeze," Snape terrifies and intimidates his students. He looks like the quintessential pantomime villain. But in the Harry Potter series, looks are often deceiving.

Snape is actually the most complex character in the books. He is deliciously enigmatic, his every action open to interpretation. Does he taunt Harry and publicly correct his mistakes because he hates him, or is he trying to ensure that Harry never forgets what he needs to know in order to survive? Has he truly renounced his association with Voldemort's murderous Death Eaters, or is he preparing to serve Harry up on a platter for the Dark Lord? Is he Dumbledore's spy,  Voldemort's spy or only interested in saving his own neck? So artfully has Rowling built up Snape's ambiguity that, even though we see him dispatch Dumbledore with the killing curse in *Harry Potter and the Half-Blood Prince*, it's hard to believe our eyes. After all, Dumbledore's trust in Snape never wavered. And, in those final moments, Dumbledore almost seemed to *ask* Snape to kill him. What else is going on here that we can't see? Time (and the sneaky Rowling) may prove me as dead wrong as Dumbledore, but I'm not ready to join Harry and say with absolute certainty that Snape is evil—are you?

Rowling has modeled Snape on more than just a nasty teacher from her childhood. He fits, amusingly and perfectly, this description of Schedoni, the charismatic villain from Ann Radcliffe's influential 1797 Gothic novel *The Italian*: "Among his associates no one loved him, many disliked him and more feared him. His figure was striking...and as he stalked along, wrapped in the black garments of his order, there was something terrible in its air; something almost super-human....An habitual gloom and severity prevailed over the deep lines of his countenance; and his eyes were so piercing that they seemed to penetrate, at a single glance, into the hearts of men and to read their most secret thoughts." In his seminal 1962 study *The Byronic Hero: Types and Prototypes*, scholar Peter L. Thorslev Jr. writes of the Gothic villain archetype, "An air of mystery is his dominant trait and characteristic of his acts. Frequently, it is increased by an aura of past secret sins." Remind you of any Potions Master you know?

A funny thing happened to the Gothic villain—readers loved him. According to Thorslev, when Gothic novels like those of Radcliffe and Horace Walpole (*The Castle of Otranto*) were adapted for the stage near the end of the eighteenth century, the Gothic villain "became gradually more sympathetic, until he appeared as half-villain, half-hero in sensibility." Lord Byron took this half-villain, half-hero as his inspiration for the passionate, flawed, darkly handsome protagonists of *The Corsair (1814), Lara (1814)* and *Manfred (1817)*. Years after Byron's death, the Brontë sisters created two of the most thrilling Byronic heroes in literature, Mr. Rochester in Charlotte's *Jane Eyre* (1846) and Heathcliff in Emily's *Wuthering Heights* (1847). Rochester and Heathcliff are moody, attractively mysterious and, above all, emotionally and psychically damaged. They are the original bad boys. They bespeak ravagement, domination, forbidden passions. And yet, encountering them on the page, our hearts fill with eternal foolish hope. Surely, these men are not bad, just sad and misunderstood, and in the hands of the right woman (putting our hands up to volunteer), they can be domesticated by love.

This is a notion that Rowling finds reprehensible. "It's a romantic but unhealthy and, unfortunately, all too common delusion of girls...that they are going to change someone," Rowling told interviewers from the Potter fan Web sites *The Leaky Cauldron* and *Mugglenet* shortly after the release of *Half-Blood Prince*. She was speaking about fans with crushes on bad boy Draco Malfoy, but she has given similar public warnings to Snape fans in the past. "Who would want Snape to be in love with them? That's a terrible idea," she said during a 1999 radio call-in interview show. Rowling describes Snape as "a gift" of a character to write but, apart from that, she gives the impression that she loathes him. Which, perhaps, makes him all the more desirable as fan fiction forbidden fruit.

ℛeader, ℐ ℱic'd ℋim

In the hands of fan fiction writers, the dark-browed and solitary Severus Snape takes his place beside Rochester and Heathcliff as a figure of powerful eroticism. We don't see Snape's sexual or romantic side in the Potter series because the story is told, almost exclusively, from Harry's point of view. But fan fiction authors have eagerly taken up the challenge of sexualizing Rowling's saga, writing between the lines like graffiti artists tempted by a pristine stretch of wall. The lack of any adult romantic partner for Snape has been particularly fertile ground for fan fiction imaginations to bloom. Some writers have seized upon Hermione as a Jane Eyre to Snape's Rochester. Others pair him with Harry in slash (homoerotic) fiction. Still others have projected themselves into the story by inventing "Mary Sue" characters[1], heroines who are dropped into the Hogwarts universe to charm the glowering serpent of Slytherin.

The first Snape-centric fan fiction, "The Love That Shattered a Man," appeared on *FanFiction.net* in 1999. It was written by one Gypsy Silverleaf, who was then in the eighth grade. An explosion of fan fiction featuring Snape as a romantic hero occurred between 2002 and 2004, roughly the period between the second and third movies and the fourth and fifth books. This newfound Snapemania was sparked in part by the casting of actor Alan Rickman—well-established as "the thinking woman's sex symbol"—in the role. Rickman's feline movements and mellifluous voice give the Potions Master a sensuality absent from the page. And beyond the shoulder-length black wig and black contact lenses Rickman wears, no attempt is made to ugly him up. Indeed, the wig and the black Victorian costume are major causes of Snape-lust; many younger fans who had never seen Rickman before glommed onto his uncanny resemblance to Goth-rock pin-up Trent Reznor from Nine Inch Nails.

Because the Harry Potter movies are coming out while the books are ongoing, it is all but impossible to separate the actors from the

43

---

[1] The online reference Wikipedia (http://en.wikipedia.org/wiki/Mary_Sue_fanfiction) offers this definition of a Mary Sue: "A pejorative expression for a fictional character who is an idealized stand-in for the author, or for a story with such a character.... The term originates in fan fiction but is spreading into general use."

characters (Rowling increasingly seems to be writing Snape's dialogue to accommodate Rickman's silken snarl). And for his longtime fans, Rickman carries many past associations into the role of Snape. His bad guys, like Hans Gruber in *Die Hard* and the Sheriff of Nottingham in *Robin Hood: Prince of Thieves*, are cruel yet irresistibly alluring. His lovers, like Colonel Brandon in *Sense and Sensibility* and Jamie in *Truly, Madly, Deeply*, are vulnerable yet frustratingly remote—Brandon is painfully reserved and Jamie is, literally, a ghost. Put that cruelty, remoteness and vulnerability together and you have the fan fiction rendering of Snape. And it's not far from the Snape of the books and movies, either. During Rowling's 2004 Edinburgh Book Festival talk, a woman in the audience exclaimed that she loved Snape, and Rowling laughed and asked, "Are you thinking about Alan Rickman or about Snape?" An excellent question. And when we figure out the answer, we'll move on to the one about the chicken or the egg.

Besides the Rickman Factor, the feverish outpouring of Snape fan fiction also had much to do with the mantle of heroic possibility Rowling drapes around Snape's shoulders at the end of *Harry Potter and the Goblet of Fire,* when Dumbledore turns to him and says, "[Y]ou know what I must ask you to do. If you are ready…if you are prepared.…" As Snape leaves for this unspecified mission, Rowling tells us that he looks "slightly paler than usual" and "his cold, black eyes glittered strangely." (Does this scene have something to do with what eventually transpires between Dumbledore and Snape in *Half-Blood Prince?*) Eager for any official evidence to justify their romanticization of the Potions Master, fan fiction writers seized that nearly wordless exchange as a confirmation that Dumbledore was sending Snape off to spy on Voldemort. Countless post-*Goblet* fics place Snape unequivocally on the side of good and have him flirting with danger as Dumbledore's mole within the Death Eaters.

Fan fiction writers found further justification for making Snape a sympathetic anti-hero in *Harry Potter and the Order of the Phoenix,* when Harry penetrates Snape's mind during Occlumency lessons and later sneaks a look at his worst memory, which has been left in Dumbledore's Pensieve. In these scenes, we (and Harry) glimpse

Snape's secret shame as an apparently abused child and an outcast, bullied teenager. Fan fiction writers believed they finally had the canonical keys to explain, if not excuse, Snape's actions as a damaged adult. (As of this writing, it's too early to gauge the effect the bombshells dropped in *Half-Blood Prince* will have on Snape fan fiction.)

There are two prevailing fan fiction interpretations of Snape, which I'll call Bastard Snape and Softie Snape. The dry-witted, elegantly sardonic Bastard Snape, best exemplified in Veresna Ussep's astringent, beautifully written stories (especially "Love's Labours, Paradise Lost"), tilts more to the Gothic villain (he won't say "I love you" after a shag). Softie Snape, who appears most memorably in white raven's compulsively readable "Tea with the Black Dragon" and Rickfan37's florid "Snape in Love," is more Byronic (he's stormy, but he'll snuggle). The various Bastard Snapes and Softie Snapes in adult fan fiction, though, all share the following characteristics (in addition to the secretiveness, sarcasm, strictness, pettiness, arrogance, intelligence and hyper-sensitivity displayed by Rowling's Snape):

45

- ◆ highly sensual; an expert lover
- ◆ sexually and emotionally sadistic; spanks students/lovers and engages in other scenarios of dominance and submission
- ◆ formal and decorous
- ◆ reflective, sometimes even guilty, about past sins
- ◆ unambiguously on the side of good
- ◆ mentally and physically tough under torture (by Voldemort and/ or Lucius Malfoy)
- ◆ prefers his paramours young, and is often paired with Hermione
- ◆ capable of deep emotion, even love, but not always willing to express or admit it
- ◆ redeemable
- ◆ incredibly well-endowed

It isn't hard to see from where some of these fan fiction characterizations and themes originate. The recurring images of Snape manfully enduring torture, for example, spring from the graveyard scene in *Goblet of Fire*, in which a resurrected Voldemort metes out the terrible Cruciatus Curse to disloyal followers. Although Snape is not present in this scene, it follows that he would be tortured if Voldemort suspected that he was a spy (his role as a spy becomes explicit in *Order of the Phoenix*).

The idea that Snape can be redeemed is a Byronic (or, perhaps, Brontëan) touch, but it is neither sappy (well, okay, maybe a little) nor pulled out of thin air. During the previously mentioned 1999 radio interview, one reader asked a question about Snape's "redemptive pattern" (this, after only the first three Potter books had been published). "I'm slightly stunned that you said that," answered Rowling cryptically, "and you'll find out why I'm so stunned if you read book seven." Call me delusional, but I agree with the fan fiction writers who explore Snape's "redemptive pattern"; it's there in the books, if you want to see it. Snape does keep saving Harry's neck (albeit never in overt or decisive ways). And in *Half-Blood Prince*, we finally learn the reason he left the Death Eaters and a possible explanation for why Dumbledore trusts him—Snape felt remorse over playing a part (inadvertently, he claims) in the murder of Harry's parents, James and Lily.

Before you echo Professor Lupin's, "Dumbledore believed Snape was sorry James was dead? Snape *hated* James...," from book six, notice where Rowling cuts off that remark. Snape did not hate Lily. He never utters a word about her throughout the series, though he freely disses James. Even before that subtle clue in *Half-Blood Prince*, there was a subset of Snape fan fiction that made Lily the love of his life and her death the crux of his conversion to the side of good. Rowling may dismiss this Snape-can-be-changed stuff as more "unhealthy" girly dreaming, but fans recognize in Snape's arc all the ingredients for a classic journey of redemption. Fan fiction depicts Snape undergoing all manner of hell, some self-inflicted, to atone for his past. It remains to be seen whether Rowling (and Harry) will deem Snape as worthy of redemption and forgiveness as fan fiction writers have.

As for the Snape/Hermione pairing... well, okay, here's one of those points on which fan fiction writers might be a little bit, er, out there. But let us not judge. The Snape/Hermione romance is based in part on schoolyard lore: If a boy picks on a girl (and vice versa), it means he likes her. In the Harry Potter books, Hermione is the *only* female student whom Snape singles out for verbal abuse and humiliation ("That is the second time you have spoken out of turn, Miss Granger...five more points from Gryffindor for being an insufferable know-it-all," Snape tells Hermione in *Harry Potter and the Prisoner of Azkaban*). And if Snape verbally disciplines and humiliates students, maybe he would physically discipline and humiliate them as well. There are so many fan fiction scenes of Snape spanking a nubile (and increasingly excited) student, they start to blur. But they pretty much all have a stirring moment like the one in "The Tenth Rule" by Pelagian, where Snape says, "Prepare yourself for your punishment, Miss Pearson! Remove the lab-coat, remove your underwear, lift your skirt and then bend over one of the desks!"

The fan fiction obsession with Snape as a disciplinarian seems to be knotted up with the desire to see him holding sway over lovers at least half his age. (According to calculations made on the *Harry Potter Lexicon* Web site, based on what is known about the ages of characters who were his classmates at Hogwarts, Snape was thirty or thirty-one years old at the beginning of the series.) There are now whole fan fiction groups, like *Ashwinder* and *When I Kissed the Teacher*, devoted to Snape/Hermione stories, despite the fact that one of the early Snape/Hermione fics, "Pawn to Queen" by Riley, was criticized by some readers for its sex scenes between Snape and the under-age student. The author later edited the story to raise Hermione's age from sixteen to eighteen; the majority of Snape/Hermione fics now portray the insufferable know-it-all as being of legal age.

47

But even making Hermione (or Mary Sue characters) eighteen years old doesn't change the balance of power in Snape fan fiction; story after story places a sexually curious student, apprentice or ward under Snape's tutelage and—at least until the clever child turns the tables—under his command. Detention, punishment, deflowering and, sometimes, true (and monogamous) love ensue. Here's a representative scene from "Tea with the Black Dragon," depicting the romantic tension between Snape and a beautiful, feisty seventh-year student who has just finished scrubbing a pile of cauldrons during one of her frequent detentions: "'You may go, Miss Draven. We are finished here....' When she finally looked up at him, the grey eyes were turbulent. He stiffened with shock when she placed her hands on his arms, stood on tiptoe and leaned into him....He could do nothing to hide the painful erection that was his immediate response as she pressed her cheek against his and breathed into his ear, 'Thank you, Professor! Thank you so much!'"

Without the constraints of "family-friendly" entertainment to which the Potter books and movies must adhere, adult fan fiction is free to state the obvious: That Snape is the very model of that enduring sexual fantasy object, the stern, older, male authority figure. This is all made even kinkier by the fact that, using the Lexicon's calculation of Snape's age, Alan Rickman is twenty-five years older than the character he plays. But the little girls understand. "Give us a detention, Mr. Rickman," read a sign held by young female fans at the London premiere of the movie *Prisoner of Azkaban*.

While we're on the subject of discipline and domination, let's talk about the sex in Snape fan fiction. It's never vanilla. And it always features one or more of the following scenes: Snape initiating the woman into S/M play; the woman kneeling before Snape to perform oral sex; the fetishization of the many buttons on Snape's frock coat, vest and trousers (this outfit, by the way, is an invention of the movies' costume designer; the books only describe his professorial robes); Snape intimately bathing the woman or otherwise insisting that she be clean; magical sex involving spells and potions; anal sex. One can only assume that fan fiction Snape's dom preferences (and cleanliness fetish) were extrapolated from the Potions Master's sadistic, exacting classroom manner in the books—Rowling's Snape truly is one of the most note-perfect S/M figures in literature, even if we're not supposed to notice. Finally, as to why the Snape of fan fiction always has such an absurdly large penis, well, you know what they say: Big nose, big...wand.

Who Owns Severus Snape?

In general, Rowling has taken a "live and let live" attitude toward fan fiction—as long as it's G-rated. In 2002, solicitors acting on behalf of Rowling, her literary agency and Warner Bros. began sending cease and desist letters to several adult fan fiction sites demanding that they remove "pornographic or sexually explicit" Harry Potter stories (*FanFiction.net* removed all of its NC-17 content in response to the letters). However, in 2004, Rowling issued a friendlier statement through her literary agency saying that she was "flattered" by Potter fan fiction, as long as it was not written for profit and as long as adult-oriented stories were not accessible to children.

Rowling has been remarkably patient, considering how difficult it must be to create in a fishbowl, with every tiny detail of her series scrutinized and debated. And it must be particularly difficult knowing that thousands and thousands of amateur writers are out there playing around inside her characters' heads. While Rowling nailed down the plot of her series several years ago, she is hampered by the creaky wheels of the traditional publishing machinery. Isn't there a chance that a fan fiction writer will get to where Rowling is going before she does?

There have already been a couple of close calls. In *Order of the Phoenix,* the vibe between the insolent Harry and the dominating Snape during their private Occlumency lessons—they knock each other around from the force of their mind-meld—echoes Snape and Harry's S/M *pas de deux* from the legendary 2001 slash fic "Happy Pothead and the Fornicating Phoenix" by Rune Scriptor (long deleted from *AdultFanFiction.net*). Snape's harsh mastery of Harry in *Order of the Phoenix* also mirrors Bastard Snape's treatment of his concubine Rosalind in Veresna Ussep's "Love's Labours, Paradise Lost." In Ussep's story, Snape tells Rosalind, "The only time that you are allowed to address me by my first name is when we are in bed....At all other times you are to address me as 'Professor' or 'Sir.'" In the "Occlumency" chapter of *Order of the Phoenix* (published five months after Ussep's story was posted), Snape tells Harry, "This may not be an ordinary class, Potter...but I am still your teacher and you will therefore call me 'Sir' or 'Professor' at all times."

Of course, Rowling's manuscript had been delivered long before "Love's Labours, Paradise Lost" was published. But the similarity, though small, illustrates how deeply some fan fiction writers understand Snape and how intuitively they have grasped the mechanics of writing him. The official Snape and the fan fiction Snape move even closer together in *Half-Blood Prince*. In chapter two ("Spinner's End"), Rowling breaks with her use of Harry's point of view to allow us to finally see the Potions Master through our own eyes. He is away from Hogwarts, in his own home, which, as in numerous fan fiction, is lined floor to ceiling with books. Snape is sophisticated, dry-witted and elegantly mannered as he entertains a distraught Narcissa Malfoy (who is seeking his protection for her son Draco) and her sister Bellatrix Lestrange (who suspects Snape of being Dumbledore's spy). Snape smoothly dominates the women in conversation, even subduing the aggressively insinuating Bellatrix with flawlessly logical, subtly sardonic explanations (shades of Bastard Snape). Erotic currents pass between Snape and Narcissa; at one point she even kneels at his feet (no doubt causing many fan fiction readers to stroke out), as she begs for his help.

50

There is Gothic romance heat in the way Rowling writes the exchanges between Snape and Narcissa: "When Snape said nothing, Narcissa seemed to lose what little self-restraint she still possessed. Standing up, she staggered to Snape and seized the front of his robes. Her face close to his, her tears falling on his chest, she gasped, 'You could do it.'" Later, when Snape makes an Unbreakable Vow with Narcissa, Rowling heaps kindling on the bonfire: With "his black eyes... fixed upon Narcissa's tear-filled blue ones," Snape kneels opposite her, their hands clasped together and bound by "a thin tongue of brilliant flame." In this chapter, we suddenly see a suave, confident, darkly attractive Snape who may even be showing a glimmer of feeling for a damsel in distress. And at the climax of the book, when Snape keeps his Unbreakable Vow (or Vows, perhaps?), kills Dumbledore and spirits Draco away to (presumed) safety, he appears more Byronic, more tragically caught in a web of intrigue, more strangely heroic than ever. In short, he has become very much like the Snape of fan fiction.

This is not to suggest that Rowling has been influenced by those she has influenced, or has made a conscious decision to give (some) fans what they want. Rather, Rowling's more mature depiction of Snape in *Half-Blood Prince* (as well as the book's emphasis on relationships and snogging among the kids) may simply mark the series' inevitable coming of age; as Harry approaches adulthood, the world suddenly opens up and he becomes aware of new facets of himself and the people around him. For years, the subversive daydreams of Potter fan fiction have enhanced and deepened adult enjoyment of what are, nominally, children's books. But the more adult tone and themes of *Half-Blood Prince* nearly bridge the gap between Rowling's series and fan fiction.

However, Rowling cannot erase what the fan fiction versions of her characters have come to mean to so many readers. At the Edinburgh Book Festival, Rowling seemed rattled when that woman proclaimed her love for Snape. "Why do you love him? Why do people love Snape?" Rowling asked the audience. "I do not understand this. Again, it's bad boy syndrome, isn't it? ... Girls, stop going for the bad guy. Go for a nice man in the first place." Rowling's frustration at having her characters misinterpreted by fans is understandable. On the page, authors have godlike control over their characters, but they can't presume to have the same control over the way readers *feel* about them. And that's what fan fiction is all about—the release of feelings. Readers have always fallen in love with fictional characters, many of whom are not "nice" (Dracula, anyone?). The Internet has merely made these literary crushes and fantasies public, made the idea of ownership too messy and passionate for any strict legal interpretation to convey. Like it or not, authors and fans make up two points of a romantic triangle. And down in his dungeon, Severus Snape's black eyes glitter avidly as he draws back the curtains of his four-poster bed and settles in for the *ménage à trois*. You will call him "Sir" at all times.

51

JOYCE MILLMAN has been writing about television and pop culture for twenty-five years. She was a finalist for the Pulitzer Prize in criticism in 1989 and 1991 for columns written while she was the television critic for the *San Francisco Examiner*. Her essays have also appeared in the *New York Times*, *Variety*, Salon.com and the *Boston Phoenix*. She is a contributor to the Smart Pop anthologies *Alias Assumed* and *Flirting with Pride and Prejudice*. In preparation for this essay, she spent many months reading Snape fan fiction. It was a dirty job, but someone had to do it.

MARGUERITE KRAUSE

Harry Potter and the End of Religion

BELIEF VERSUS KNOWLEDGE, FAITH VERSUS THOUGHT. THE DIS-
AGREEMENT BETWEEN THE TWO CAMPS GOES BACK, IN ALL LIKE-
LIHOOD, TO THE CAVES. WHO WOULD HAVE THOUGHT THAT A
SET OF CHILDREN'S BOOKS WOULD TURN INTO YET ANOTHER BAT-
TLEGROUND FOR THE TWO SIDES? PERHAPS BECAUSE HARRY IS
AN EXAMPLE OF THAT MOST DANGEROUS OF EXAMPLES: SOMEONE
LEARNING TO THINK FOR HIMSELF.

*I*S HARRY POTTER A DANGER to the spiritual health of today's children and a threat to the moral fabric of contemporary society?

Well...that depends.

To sincere followers of conservative Christian traditions, the answer to this question is a clear and unequivocal "Yes!"
The publication of J. K. Rowling's *Harry Potter and the Sorcerer's Stone*
(and each subsequent volume in the series) inspired a strident outpouring of criticism from individuals and organizations dedicated
to protecting impressionable young minds from the evil influences
of Satanism, witchcraft and the increasing godlessness of the modern world. Opponents of the books declare that parents who expose
their children to the magical adventures of Harry and his friends are
condemning them to eternal torment in the fires of Hell. To hear
these critics talk, to enjoy Rowling's fictional universe is to contribute to the ultimate collapse of Western Civilization as we know it.

One glance at the sales figures for the Harry Potter novels, not to mention the box office receipts for the hugely successful feature films, suggests that only a small minority of people have decided to stay away from Harry for the sake of their immortal souls. It's tempting to simply dismiss commentaries posted on religiously conservative Web sites, or diatribes published in the mainstream media, as the ravings of fundamentalist religious fanatics. Surely their arguments are irrelevant to anyone who doesn't follow their belief systems.

Or are they?

What, exactly, is so bad about Harry Potter? Are Rowling's stories as potentially dangerous as their detractors claim them to be? And if you don't subscribe to the same beliefs as the people who denounce the books as evil, why should you care?

The likelihood that religion plays a part in your life varies widely depending on where you live, how old you are and whose statistical studies you're consulting for your information. It also depends, significantly, on how you define the word "religion." My pocket dictionary calls religion "an organized system of belief and ritual centering on a supernatural being or beings." Sounds simple and straightforward . . . until you start wondering about the words within the definition. An "organized system"—okay, that's pretty self-explanatory. But what is belief? What constitutes ritual? Who decides the difference between natural and supernatural?

Here at the beginning of the twenty-first century, having faith in a deity or deities (the supernatural, in one form or another) is still the norm in many cultures, especially in the developing countries of the Third World. In developed, industrialized nations, Americans tend to affiliate with organized religions more often than do citizens of similar levels of education and economic status in Europe, Canada and Australia. But even people who don't consider themselves particularly religious, or don't identify with any specific historical tradition of faith and ritual, are likely to have strong opinions about religious subjects. You don't have to be a practicing Buddhist, church-going Methodist or observant Jew to find yourself wondering about the nature of good and evil, how the world was created, why you were born or what happens after you die.

Religious feeling—spirituality—seems to be innate in human beings, as much a part of our basic nature as our ability to acquire language, walk bipedally and manipulate the world around us with our opposable thumbs. In fact, the capacity for spirituality may be a defining human trait. Prehistoric populations are identified as fully human—or not—based in part on the presence or absence of cave drawings, carved figurines, ritualized burial of the dead or other signs of spiritual self-expression. In cultures around the world and throughout history, humans have sought to find meaning and structure in the universe. Again and again, despite the evidence all around us—earthquake, flood, war, disease—humans dream of an ideal state of existence where justice prevails. Despite our flaws, we envision perfection. Despite our mortality, we imagine eternity.

How do we come up with such ideas? More importantly—why? Is it possible that human beings are born with a religious instinct? If so, what purpose could it possibly serve? Is it proof that we are creatures of spirit as well as mere flesh and blood? Or is it merely an odd side-effect of the basic biochemical functioning of our brains?

55

The trouble with questions regarding religion is that they rarely come with definitive, objectively verifiable answers. Maybe the answers aren't as important as the questions themselves. But this leads to other problems. Although similar questions occur to most of us at one time or another, that's no guarantee that we'll come up with similar answers. History is full of examples of people finding it impossible to agree on the "correct" way to express common religious feelings, and the frequently violent outcomes of such disagreements—persecution, political upheaval, all-out war.

Which leads us back to our original question: Why do certain self-described religious people—specifically conservative, traditionalist Christians—get so upset about Harry Potter? And do their concerns have any relevance for people who don't share their particular beliefs?

For much of the past two thousand years, Christianity has played a central role in world history, as well as in the private lives of countless millions of people. Christian symbols, practices, rhetoric and philosophy provide the underpinning for modern Western culture at such a fundamental level that many people, Christian and non-Christian alike, barely notice their presence. Because of the way Christianity pervades our society, even if you've never set foot inside a church you're still likely to be familiar with at least a few Christian concepts: the existence of a single, all-powerful God; Jesus as the savior of the faithful; the idea that prayers will be heard and answered by God.

It's important to recognize that each subdivision within the Christian community—Roman Catholic, Greek Orthodox, Coptic, Lutheran, Baptist, Evangelical, Church of England, Jehovah's Witness, Presbyterian, sect after sect too numerous to list here—has its own individual interpretation of the stories recorded in the Christian Bible, adding and subtracting teachings and rituals based on spiritual revelations received by key leaders and handed down from generation to generation. This helps explain why there hasn't been a unified, worldwide uprising of Christian protest against Harry Potter; lots of Christians think the stories are at worst harmless entertainment or at best useful tools for teaching moral and ethical values to children.

56

On the surface, Harry and his friends are Christians, living in a Christian society. Christmas—a major Christian religious holiday—is celebrated at Hogwarts. The holiday's traditions, as described in affectionate detail by Rowling, include gift-giving, decorating with evergreen trees and mistletoe, feasts and, at least for the Weasley family, listening to music on the radio on Christmas Eve. The "holiday spirit" evoked in the books is comfortably familiar to anyone who has ever lived in a dominantly Christian community:

> The Hogwarts staff, demonstrating a continued desire to impress the visitors from Beauxbatons and Durmstrang, seemed determined to show the castle at its best this Christmas. When the decorations went up, Harry noticed that they were the most stunning he had yet seen inside the school. Everlasting icicles had been attached to the banisters of the marble staircase; the usual twelve Christmas trees in the Great Hall were bedecked with everything from luminous holly berries to real, hooting, golden owls, and the suits of armor had all been bewitched to sing carols whenever anyone passed them. (*Harry Potter and the Goblet of Fire*)

Sounds lovely, doesn't it? But Rowling's depiction of Christmas is all surface, no substance. In book after book, the trappings of Christianity are used as just another sort of background scenery, like the landscape or the weather. They have no meaningful content. The passage quoted above continues:

> It was quite something to hear "O Come, All Ye Faithful" sung by an empty helmet that only knew half the words. Several times, Filch the caretaker had to extract Peeves from inside the armor, where he had taken to hiding, filling in the gaps in the songs with lyrics of his own invention, all of which were very rude. (*Goblet of Fire*)

One reason a sincere Christian might object to Rowling's stories is their failure to present Christianity as a vibrant religion, relevant to the daily lives of its followers. None of Rowling's characters ever talk (or even think) about Jesus, or the Bible, or salvation. Nowhere in any of the books, at Christmas or any other season of the year, do any of the characters go to church. This isn't just a choice of certain individuals or families. The students at Hogwarts never go to chapel. For all we can tell from the descriptions given in the books, the school doesn't even have a chapel. Daily announcements and special ceremonial occasions alike take place in the Great Hall. The description of Harry's Christmas with the Weasleys in *Harry Potter and the Half-Blood Prince* includes no mention of attending church services, although that could be interpreted as merely the custom of one particular family. However, from the very beginning of the series we have been presented with the example of a model, "average" family, the Dursleys:

57

> Mrs. and Mrs. Dursley, of number four, Privet Drive, were proud to say that they were perfectly normal, thank you very much. They were the last people you'd expect to be involved in anything strange or mysterious, because they just didn't hold with such nonsense. (*Sorcerer's Stone*)

If church attendance was the norm for respectable people in the world of Harry Potter, you would think that the Dursleys would be prominent members of their local congregation. Yet on Privet Drive, as at Hogwarts, no mention of church services or church officials— ministers, priests, reverends, deacons—is ever made.

But the primary reason that some people object to Harry Potter— or at least the one most often strongly voiced—is based on a literal reading of the Christian Bible. Several passages (Deuteronomy 18:10–12 and Exodus 22:17, for example) instruct the ancient Israelites to abstain from practicing witchcraft or consorting with anyone who does. For centuries, these verses have provided the foundation for the Christian definition of "magic" as evil.

Yet today, not all Christians approach Scripture literally. Some regard the Bible as a unique and highly valuable collection of very old texts—histories, poems, parables, prophecies—first put down in written form anywhere from two to three to four thousand years ago (depending on which scholarly source you consult), in languages such as ancient Hebrew, Aramaic and Greek. In the centuries since

then, those original texts have been translated and retranslated into almost all of the languages on Earth. Anyone who has ever studied a foreign language knows how difficult it can be to translate words and ideas from one language to another. Inconsistencies in wording—and changes in meaning—inevitably crop up. Students of the Bible who are aware of this challenge examine the text with the goal of gaining a deeper, richer understanding of its message by acquiring a comprehensive knowledge of its origins and the various permutations it has gone through over the centuries.

For literalist Christians, however, if the Bible says witchcraft is "an abomination," then it's an abomination. No scholarly exploration of the language and socioeconomic conditions of the ancient culture in which the Bible's code of morality originated makes a difference to that fundamental truth.

Another factor to keep in mind is that Christians today are practicing a religion shaped by two thousand years of history and tradition. The full saga of Christianity's conflict with the polytheistic religions it encountered as it spread across Europe is too complex to relate here. Suffice it to say that the resulting culture clash profoundly affected all concerned. Sometimes the Church took symbols or rituals from local pagan traditions and reinterpreted them to convey Christian messages. In other cases, instead of adapting polytheistic practices to its own needs, the Church labeled them as evil. Old gods were declared to be demons, which meant that to worship in the old way—to seek to communicate with deities other than the Christian God—was, by definition, consorting with demons. The only acceptable way to approach the supernatural was through Christian ritual and Christian prayer. Anything else was magic, witchcraft, superstition—and thus forbidden.

To this day, some people worry that Christianity is in competition with other religions, including various forms of paganism. Although some Christians call their pagan rivals "Wiccans" or "modern witches," others use the broad term "occult" to encompass everything they abhor. For literalist Christians, everything associated with the practices mentioned in the Bible as "detestable to the Lord," including spells, levitation, fortune telling and supernatural beings, are works of darkness to be shunned. Rowling's books contain all those things. That makes the Harry Potter books works of darkness, dangerous because they defy the strictures of Christian morality and encourage readers to accept pagan religious practices as "normal."

The trouble with this conclusion is that practicing pagans insist that Rowling's books do *not* portray pagan religious practices or represent their beliefs. The Harry Potter universe may be full of witches and wizards who wave magic wands and fly around on broomsticks but, according to modern pagans, all these are simply dramatic elements in a work of fiction with no relation whatsoever to any contemporary religious practice.

The truth is, Harry and his friends don't practice witchcraft as a religion any more than they practice Christianity as a religion. They don't engage in public worship or private prayer of any kind. Thoughts of God, or gods, never cross their minds. Even when discussing what we usually think of as "religious" subjects, such as questions of good and evil or the nature of the soul, there is no sign that the characters in the books believe in the existence of any sort of deity:

59

[Quirrell:] "A foolish young man I was then, full of ridiculous ideas about good and evil. Lord Voldemort showed me how wrong I was. There is no good and evil, there is only power, and those too weak to seek it...." (*Sorcerer's Stone*)

"Well, you split your soul, you see," said Slughorn, "and hide part of it in an object outside the body. Then, even if one's body is attacked or destroyed, one cannot die, for part of the soul remains earthborn and undamaged.... You must understand that the soul is supposed to remain intact and whole. Splitting it is an act of violation, it is against nature." (*Half-Blood Prince*)

Note the wording: "against nature." Not "heresy" or "an abomination" or any other phrase that would imply that the act is prohibited because it defies rules laid down by God.

60

Literalist Christians who brand Harry a dangerous role model for children because he is not a Christian (arguably true), or because he actively promotes a competing religion (arguably false), are missing the point. Harry and his friends, through all their adventures and personal growth and intellectual discoveries, demonstrate time and again that they have no interest in or need for any kind of religion at all.

Over the course of the books, Harry confronts many questions that traditionally have fallen into the realm of religious or spiritual concerns. Yet the answers he finds have nothing to do with religion—no "organized systems," no "beliefs," no "supernatural being or beings."

For instance, one of Harry's recurring questions is what happens to people after they die:

[Dumbledore:] "After all, to the well-organized mind, death is but the next great adventure." (*Sorcerer's Stone*)

[Dumbledore:] "You think the dead we loved ever truly leave us? You think that we don't recall them more clearly than ever in times of great trouble? Your father is alive in you, Harry, and shows himself most plainly when you have need of him." (*Harry Potter and the Prisoner of Azkaban*)

"Wizards can leave an imprint of themselves upon the earth, to walk palely where their living selves once trod," said Nick miserably. "But very few wizards choose that path.... [referring to Sirius] He will have...gone on."

"What d'you mean, 'gone on'?" said Harry quickly. "Gone on where? Listen—what happens when you die, anyway? Where do you go? Why doesn't everyone come back? Why isn't this place full of ghosts? Why—?"

"I was afraid of death," said Nick. "I chose to remain behind. I sometimes wonder whether I oughtn't to have.... Well, that is neither here nor there.... In fact, *I* am neither here nor there...." He gave a small, sad chuckle. "I know nothing of the secrets of death, Harry, for I chose my feeble imitation of life instead." (*Harry Potter and the Order of the Phoenix*)

[Luna:] "And anyway, it's not as though I'll never see Mum again, is it?"

"Er—isn't it?" said Harry uncertainly.

She shook her head in disbelief. "Oh, come on. You heard them, just behind the veil, didn't you?"

"You mean...."

"In that room with the archway. They were just lurking out of sight, that's all. You heard them." (*Order of the Phoenix*)

In Harry's world, there is no heaven waiting for the righteous or hell waiting for evildoers. No one mentions the possibility of rebirth or reincarnation. Yet everyone clearly believes that people possess a "soul" and that, after the mortal body dies, the immortal soul goes on—they just don't know where. Nor, for the most part, do they seem to care. Harry's interest in the subject is atypical, and entirely personal. His wish that he might have known his parents and his grief over the death of Sirius lead him to wonder if, and when, he might see them again. Unfortunately for Harry, no one has a definitive answer for his questions about the ultimate destiny of the human soul, so his curiosity remains unsatisfied.

However, Harry's questions about what happens after a person dies are noteworthy not for the answers he finds, or fails to find, but for the approach he takes. Whenever Harry and his friends encounter a mystery, they follow a similar pattern in trying to solve it. They discuss the matter together, to see if one of them can suggest a solution based on their existing knowledge and experiences. If that doesn't work, they seek additional information and assistance from outside sources, such as their classroom textbooks, the school library or helpful teachers like Hagrid. At moments of crisis, however, each of them—and Harry especially—tends to turn to the greatest source of power in Rowling's universe: personal courage and inner strength.

Religion in Harry Potter's world is not merely irrelevant; it literally doesn't exist. There is no divine being to pray to, no "higher power" from which to seek guidance or strength. Power, moral and physical, lies within the individual and is wielded according to the natural laws of Rowling's universe. None of the characters, whether good or evil, express any belief in the supernatural. Magic spells and magical creatures abound in the Harry Potter universe as entirely natural phenomena. Witches and wizards use magic the way engineers and architects here in the twenty-first century use mathematics or physics: as tools with which the human mind can conceive new ideas and manipulate the physical world. For witches as for engineers, an individual's skill, training, ingenuity and simple hard work can enable her to achieve better results than her less-talented peers. Harry and his friends recognize that magical talent varies widely, ranging from the entirely ungifted Muggles at one end of the spectrum to the most powerful wizards—Dumbledore and Voldemort—at the other. But Dumbledore and Voldemort are neither demons nor gods. They are simply people who happened to be born with a level of magical ability, later enhanced by years of training and personal dedication and ambition, that others lack. Although many in the wizarding world are terrified of Voldemort, and his followers serve him slavishly, Rowling makes it clear that his abilities are not supernatural. He is an immensely powerful, dangerous, evil man—but still a man. Practically speaking, there is no fundamental difference between Lord Voldemort and his minions, or between Dumbledore and a Squib like Filch or between any magic-user and the most oblivious Muggle. All are human beings. The only consistent difference between individuals in Rowling's books is what use they make of the power they possess.

And herein lies the real ethical challenge posed by Harry Potter. It's not that Harry is a bad Christian role model, or that he promotes a Wiccan agenda or tempts anyone to worship Satan. It's that, in Harry's world, the characters make their own, independent moral choices, with no reference to any established, higher moral authority—no church, no Bible, no God. Harry turns to his friends and to a few trusted elders like Sirius, Hagrid and Dumbledore for support and occasional advice but, ultimately, the decisions he makes are based on his personal understanding of right and wrong, good and evil.

Furthermore, in Harry's world, there is no outside, objective scale by which to evaluate a person's choices. Right and wrong are subjective, changing with the situation. Harry, for example, prefers to speak the truth. Yet again and again throughout the books he lies to his teachers, his friends, Dumbledore, representatives from the Ministry of Magic—anyone at all, in fact, if he's convinced that lying is the best way to accomplish his goals. Objectively, there seems to be little difference between Harry and Draco Malfoy, who also frequently and skillfully practices deception to achieve his ends.

Authorities, in the form of individuals and institutions, do exist in the Harry Potter universe. But Rowling makes it clear that it is unwise to obey a rule or follow a leader just because they are authoritative. The Ministry of Magic oversees affairs in the wizarding world, passing and enforcing laws that, theoretically at least, are intended to enable witches and wizards to live peaceably with one another and with the wider Muggle community. The Ministry, however, makes mistakes. Cornelius Fudge jeopardizes everyone's safety by refusing to believe that Lord Voldemort has returned. Dolores Umbridge is a Ministry official, yet she tortures Harry simply because she is a petty, egotistical, vicious human being. Other authority figures prove equally, dangerously fallible. Voldemort, revered by his followers as the highest authority in his area of specialization—dark magic—is hindered repeatedly in his quest for power

63

by his mishandling of situations and misjudgment of individuals. Even Albus Dumbledore, respected by his friends and feared by his enemies, is not perfect. Despite his age, experience and wisdom he occasionally makes the wrong decision. Some of his poor choices cause inconvenience or unhappiness for the people around him; from Harry's point of view, his worst mistake—trusting Severus Snape—results in his death.

Harry Potter can be considered a dangerous role model for children because, for Harry, the highest moral authority is the inner prompting of his own heart and mind. He can't turn to his society's government, the Ministry of Magic, for guidance, because it is full of corrupt officials and inept, cumbersome bureaucracy. And he can't depend on the parental figures in his life, because all of them are flawed. His parents fail him by dying before he has a chance to know them. The Dursleys are narrowminded and cruel; Hagrid, not too bright; Sirius, short-tempered and impulsive; Dumbledore, too willing to trust and love.

Harry decides life's most critical ethical questions for himself. The nature of good and evil is not defined for him by religious teachings; "evil" is not spelled out as the Satanism of Christianity or the dark half of a Zoroastrian-style duality theology, or any other clear, easy-to-recognize dogma. Instead, Harry and all the other characters assess for themselves what is "right" and what is "wrong." As the story progresses, Rowling does draw a clear distinction between which characters she considers to be good and which bad. However, no reason is given to justify a person's inclusion in either category; apparently it is considered self-evident, to both the characters and the reader. (Except, of course, in the case of intentionally ambiguous characters.) Thus, Voldemort and his followers are evil because they are cruel and greedy and cause pain to others. Harry and his friends are good because they are kind and generous and supportive of others. Someone like Fudge is judged to be good when he is acting in his capacity as a law-enforcing minister, but bad when he acts in opposition to Dumbledore. And then there is Snape, the classic double agent. We are never sure what to expect from him or how to react to him. Should we dislike Snape for what may be all the wrong reasons:

his greasy hair, his unsavory past, his animosity toward Harry? Or should we trust him for what may *also* be the wrong reasons: our respect for Dumbledore's judgment, pity for the way Snape was bullied at school, the fact that he protects Harry on certain occasions, hope that repentance can be genuine?

There's an element of risk in such morally confusing messages. With no clear guidelines, what's to prevent an innocent young reader from drawing the wrong conclusions about various incidents and characters in the Harry Potter saga? Furthermore, what happens to the smooth operation of institutions that rely on the unquestioning obedience of their members if people start believing that they, like Harry, should be able to make important moral judgments and life decisions for themselves?

This, perhaps, is the most disturbing, and potentially threatening, concept in Rowling's universe: that each person is completely responsible for his or her own fate. Although certain circumstances are outside the control of an individual character (no one can choose their parents, or the circumstances of their childhoods), the way each person responds to events is entirely up to them. Individuals must live with the consequences of their actions. There is no appeal to a supernatural power for mercy, no promise of divine justice. God is not poised to step in and make everything all right, like the cavalry coming over the hill in the nick of time. There are only good people, like Harry and his friends, trying to protect themselves and their families from bad people, like the Malfoys and Voldemort. And all any of them have to rely on is their own inner strength and skills and courage.

The trouble with this philosophy of personal choice and self-reliance is that, translated into everyday life, it flies against the principles on which contemporary society is based. Human communities rely on the cooperation and, yes, obedience of their members in order to function. Authorities, in the form of religious leaders, elected officials and public safety personnel, establish and enforce the rule of law. Priests and pastors tell us we must not steal or commit adultery. The fire chief tells construction companies how many and what size windows they have to provide in bedrooms in the homes they build.

65

The city council tells us we can't dump our sewage into the street. The police tell us we can't drive drunk.

Sadly, history teaches that, in the absence of recognized and respected authority, community order breaks down. Many people seem to feel that if a law can't be enforced, they're free to break it. Looters in towns devastated by a natural disaster are a perfect example. So are corporate executives who enrich themselves at the expense of their company's shareholders, with no concern over whether their action is right or wrong, only whether or not they can get away with it. Like Harry, both looters and white-collar criminals have decided that the established rules of their respective societies don't apply to them, and therefore they can do whatever they think best.

When you look at it this way, it starts to sound like maybe the traditionalist Christians are onto something after all. Maybe there are lessons in the Harry Potter books that *could* lead to the collapse of Western Civilization as we know it.

There's no doubt that Harry exists in a godless world. He does not believe in the omnipotence of a single deity or give any indication that religious faith has a place in his life. He defies established authority to follow his personal conscience instead. Lack of religion, however, is not the same as lack of morality. Harry and his friends *do* care, deeply, about the difference between right and wrong. For them, the question of whether a person is good or evil—the fundamental condition of their soul—is answered entirely by their actions, not by anything they profess to believe. Each individual must choose his or her own life's path: to pursue power and influence for its own sake, like Voldemort, or, like Dumbledore, to nurture the strengths and talents that grow out of love.

Because Harry's is a secular world, its residents find answers to their spiritual and ethical dilemmas without the help of religion. Individuals are expected to decide right and wrong for themselves, and they *do* decide. Where the big questions are concerned—*Who am I? How should I act? What does my life mean?*—they have to discover the answers for themselves. Harry and his friends are continuously challenged to think about their options and make choices: to avoid trouble or pursue justice, to mind their own business or risk everything for the sake of the greater good. If there's one message that surfaces again and again in the Harry Potter books, it's the importance of taking personal responsibility for the things you care about.

So, the next time you hear someone complaining that the Harry Potter books are a bad influence on children, don't just dismiss their concerns out of hand. In many ways, Harry *is* a dangerous role model. The lessons he teaches do not fit comfortably within the existing moral fabric of our society. Embracing them encourages us to change the way we think about religion, and ethics, and personal responsibility. And change, no matter its source, is always threatening.

As well as, perhaps, a reason for hope.

MARGUERITE KRAUSE'S favorite activities involve the printed word. In addition to writing, she works as a freelance copy editor, helping other writers to sharpen their skills, and for relaxation loves nothing better than to curl up with a good book. She is married to her high school sweetheart; they have two children. You can find more of Marguerite's writing in the anthologies *Seven Seasons of Buffy*, *Five Seasons of Angel* and *The Anthology at the End of the Universe*; her two-part epic fantasy, *Moons' Dreaming* and *Moons' Dancing*, co-written with Susan Sizemore; and her fantasy novel, *Blind Vision*.

ELISABETH DeVOS

It's All About God

AFICIONADOS OF SCIENCE FICTION AND FANTASY OFTEN TALK ABOUT HOW IMPORTANT THE SENSE OF WONDER IS TO THE READERS OF BOTH GENRES. ELISABETH DeVOS MAKES A TELLING ARGUMENT FOR HOW THIS IS NOT JUST IMPORTANT TO LOVERS OF THE FANTASTIC, BUT TO ALL OF US.

DOZENS OF EVANGELICAL PARENTS demand that libraries ban them. A few fundamentalist churches build bonfires with them. Meanwhile, the Harry Potter novels draw millions of readers into their magical world as irresistibly as if we were Charmed.

Why?

Not because J. K. Rowling made a deal with the Devil, as Internet rumors suggest. And not because she's luring innocent youngsters into a life of witchcraft and tree-worship, as the religious reactionaries fear.

No, the reason for Harry Potter's extraordinary rise to the top of both the bestseller and banned book lists is that we Muggles are deeply drawn to that most mythical, mystical being of all—*the one which never appears in Rowling's stories.* Our innate human drive to connect with the magical power that created us is what propels fans of Rowling's epic into its six volumes. And, ironically, that same drive energizes the fervent beliefs of its foes.

To those pious individuals, the Harry Potter books are a series of giant recruiting pamphlets for modern occultism: *The Few, the Proud, the Magical!* They are a seductive invitation to evil that glorify beliefs and practices Christianity has spent two millennia attacking with censorship and fire. And by continuing the assault, enemies of Rowling's tales acknowledge the spiritual power of her work. After all, there would be no need to banish and burn them if her novels were viewed, from the fundamentalist standpoint, as benign. Or if they were viewed, as they are by many devout defenders of the series, as fully compatible with faith.

However, everyone agrees that traditional religion, with the exception of some secularized Christian holidays, is excluded from the stories. So where does their spiritual power come from? If you ask an anti-Harry evangelical, they'll probably tell you that not only is God absent from Rowling's novels, but what is glorified instead is an unholy hybrid of paganism and Satanism, Wicca and witchcraft. A faith that draws its power from dark sources, its morality from shades of grey. A mythology that, at best, sets a bad example and, at worst, poses a grave spiritual danger to anyone misguided enough to read the books. But if we examine this perception, we notice three inconsistencies, and exploring them enables us to move toward an understanding of the true reasons for the fanatical reactions, both positive and negative, evoked by the series.

First, Satan must be in the eye of the beholder, because he is certainly *not* in the pages of Harry Potter. Six books and counting, and we've got guys riding invisible horses, horses with one horn, and horned dragons with tails, but no *invisible guy* with *horns* and a *tail*. In fact, there are no gods or godlike beings—good or evil—at all. There are no priests and priestesses (or their equivalent) ordained as the earthly emissaries of a god. There is no worship, no religious ritual, no doctrine of faith. There's not even a church or temple built in some omnipotent being's honor, just a big old academic institution with *really* interesting architecture. And the Muggles that end up at Hogwarts School of Witchcraft and Wizardry don't come by their powers as the result of conversion to a dark religious sect; they were born that way. They don't even have to pledge allegiance to magic in order to become part of the magical world; they just have to show up on time for the Hogwarts Express (or enchant an old car). In short, magic, as portrayed in Rowling's series, is not a religion, nor does it arise from one.

Which brings us to the second problem with the slippery-slope-to-Satan view of Harry Potter: Not only does its magic not displace God, but instead it is a natural science. Magic isn't something you believe in any more than we believe in gravity or electromagnetism. These forces are givens in our reality, just as magic is a given in the alternate reality of Harry Potter. And in that world, the natural magical force is the basis for technology: It powers transportation, protects buildings, cooks food and even washes the dishes.

Magical technology, like Muggle technology, is a work in progress, with the knowledge base always under expansion. In both realities, technology doesn't come cheap, and money buys advantage, as the Slytherin Quidditch team's Nimbus Two Thousand and One broomsticks, courtesy of Draco's rich dad, attest. But the underlying source of power is neutral: Magic, like any other system of knowledge, is neither good nor bad. It is how it is used that determines whether the magician is an Auror or a Death Eater.

And it is not just people who are magical in Harry Potter's hidden world—for science is simply a means of describing nature. The enchanted ecosystem is richly populated by plants, animals and some very interesting combinations thereof. It sustains a kingdom of diverse beings upon which its human inhabitants depend, just as our ability to thrive is linked to that of the creatures which share our environment.

71

Despite all this, to its fundamentalist critics Harry Potter's magic is anything *but* natural and neutral, because they believe that anyone who engages in something called or resembling witchcraft is not going to end up curled next to the Gryffindor fireplace on a cold winter evening; they're going to end up someplace very hot. But...do they really believe this? Disney, another producer of blockbuster fantasy—in particular, *Fantasia*—made millions without getting burned for its trademarked enchantment. But which is really more demonic: a leering mouse in a wizard's cap bringing on the biblical flood with an out-of-control bewitched mop, or a bunch of kids playing aerial polo on cruelty-free, non-polluting, self-powered stick ponies? And which sets a worse example: stargazing man-horses adhering to a rigid code of honor, or prancing pretty-boys pairing off with pastel bimbos?

This double standard for magic in children's entertainment is the third problem with the perception of Harry Potter as wicked: If occult or pagan content were really the issue, then the ultra-conservative Christians would have boycotted Mickey long before he instituted domestic-partnership policies. Rowling's stories, however, are not an epic animated series in book form: cute, colorized and so far removed from our world as to be utterly non-threatening. Their author does not indemnify herself by requiring us to give up our reality—or die—in order to escape to a magical place. Instead she proclaims that enchantment is all around us, just hidden from view.

And the enchanted realm of Harry Potter refuses, unlike that other mega-selling magical kingdom of children's entertainment, to eviscerate its mythical inhabitants and embalm them in cheesy cartoons, or to cower behind fairy tales that have been sanitized for mass consumption. Its wizards are not plastic figurines (at least, they didn't start out that way), nor is their wizardry glitter and harmless make-believe. Rowling does not denature the imaginings of past cultures any more than she omits the shortcomings of contemporary ones. And so her creation is a world that we intuitively recognize, one that we instantly believe: a world of true magic that rings true. This, as we will see, is why it speaks so strongly to the part of us that seeks the true magic of our own world. And why certain individuals, who believe they can only find that magic through narrow interpretation of a very different set of books, are so alarmed by its words.

72

Thus we come again to our paradox. If the Potter-purgers are wrong, and the intense temptation of Rowling's stories does not arise from unholy sources—but if God, or any semblance thereof, is noticeably absent from her novels—then from where is their spiritual power coming? And how does it account for their unprecedented success? To answer these questions, we must first recognize that while the basis of the opposition to Rowling's tales extends centuries into the past, those tales' extraordinary popularity is very much a function of the present time.

The most high-tech generation ever to walk the Earth has embraced the Harry Potter books in staggering numbers because those books are fantasy. Since World War II defined a new technological era and Tolkien's Lord of the Rings trilogy defined a new literary genre, progress has smashed everything from atoms to sacred assertions about our universe—sending readers both young and not-so-young fleeing into the pages of novels in which fireballs result from incantations and not ammunitions. The fantasy genre has exploded as once science-fictional terrors keep materializing like boggarts in the daily news and once holy lines keep vanishing like the markings on a Marauder's Map. And this is because fantasy provides an escape—from the complexity created by progress, from the oppressive rationalism that dominates modern life, and from the increasingly uneasy cohabitation of science and religion.

God lives in religion—and has a *lot* of houses. This is the impression that most of us form growing up. But like Harry traveling by Floo powder and arriving covered in ash, we arrive in our houses of worship coated with the byproducts of science: digital devices in our hands, synthetic fibers on our bodies, engineered lenses over our eyes. And that's nothing compared to the soot coating our minds. Rationalism has burned there since we were old enough to ask "why?"—a fire carefully cultivated through years of schooling, stoked stronger with every new discovery. For most of us, that fire can never be extinguished, and it daily consumes more of our worldview as mystery after mystery is illuminated by its glaring light. God may have a lot of houses, but unless they are defended by a rejection of science, their intellectual property is shrinking at an alarming rate.

What is more alarming, since those houses are not located at number twelve, Grimmauld Place, is that their property can shrink at all. What we are taught we will find in religion is that which is eternal, not that which can be made obsolete by someone's bright idea, and that which is undeniably true, not that for which we have to take someone else's word. We are also taught we will find an unfailing moral compass—not guidance that, in this era of awesome new horizons, appears centuries out of date. And most importantly, we are taught we will find connection to the ultimate magic that is God—a connection that, like a phone call made from a bad cell, is hard to maintain when the intermediary is having technical difficulties.

And so millions of high-tech kids have turned off their mobile phones and video games to actually pick up a book—a book from the most explosive fantasy series of all. Because while most epics justify the existence of magic by transporting us to a vaguely medieval past, Rowling's stories are set in a world like ours—but with an added dimension built on the very mythologies that religion and science, like two adversaries united against a common foe, have eradicated as living beliefs. And this is why legions of us so greatly identify with their young protagonist and his emancipation from stifling, magic-averse Privet Drive: Because like Harry prior to the arrival of that self-replicating letter, we too have spent our lives in a place devoid—or at least in denial—of supernatural power that we can actually perceive. A place where all forms of magic are judged by predetermined notions, and our rare innocent encounters with the paranormal are dismissed as nonsense. And so when Harry is whisked away by his hairy, half-giant rescuer, we cheer—and want desperately to go along for the ride, so that we too can escape the rigid authorities that define our existence and that make it increasingly difficult for us to connect with the miraculous force that is all around us.

And escape we do—to a place where religion is notably absent, science is marginalized and technology is a curiosity, a clumsy crutch used by the unfortunate Muggles who can't access the endless power that resides in the world within their world. It is a poor second choice to being magical, as proved by the relish with which Muggle-raised Harry and Muggle-born Hermione abandon the realm of science for a place that is every bit as dangerous. We all know that in their shoes we'd do the same, even if the alternative wasn't living in a cupboard. We want to be on the other side of the barrier at platform nine and three-quarters, where bedrooms are considerably larger and where magic may hide ancient houses and institutions but is not hidden within them. Where access to the miraculous is available now, instead of being conditioned upon a lifetime of good behavior. And where that power, although still falling far short of omnipotence, is an irrefutable *fact*.

Magical ability may not be gifted equally to everyone, but even the unfortunate, magicless Squibs still have the comfort of *knowing* that magic exists, that there is a department in the Ministry of Magic where the great mysteries of life are kept for study, as opposed to being only words and intangible experiences, the very reality of which science regularly assaults. How comforting to understand that illusions are conjured by Charms, and time is real enough to be captured in a bell jar instead of being labeled an illusion conjured by equations only mathematical geniuses will ever comprehend. How deeply reassuring to know—from personal experience—that light truly *can* be created with words. And so we identify, at last, the source of Harry Potter's spiritual appeal: Rowling's magical world, perhaps more than any other fictional realm, validates our most fundamental longing— a universal desire to access the amazing power that lets there be light and everything upon which that light shines.

It is this longing which has fueled mankind's ongoing spiritual quest and belief in stories resulting from it, many of which have become worldwide bestsellers in their own right. Crisscross continents and centuries, and you will encounter again and again not only the beings that dwell in the collective unconscious, but prophecy and rituals aimed at summoning supernatural power—the same menagerie and magic we encounter in Rowling's novels. But her inclusiveness does not evangelize the mythologies of the past: Instead, it acknowledges the common yearning that gave rise to those attempts to find and describe the magic hidden within us and our world. And more, her inclusiveness generates a new and unique mythology that comes full circle by evoking the same aspects of spiritual experience that inspired its sources. Let us now look at how:

Rowling's tales are about and written for those experiencing childhood—when awe is our natural state. But for today's children, that awareness is too often exhausted by the mind-numbing explanations and sensory overstimulations of the Technological Age. And then along came Harry Potter, offering a portal into a realm populated by mythical, mystical beings that resonate someplace deep inside us. A world where we are surrounded by the impossible, the stuff of dreams and nightmares. The amazing things that we Muggles hear tell of, or sometimes even glimpse, are out in plain view, which does not eliminate mystery as explanation but rather *confirms* mystery.

75

The world of Harry Potter is a place where something can arise from nothing, and where there is an explanation of how that doesn't rob us of our sense of wonder or require us to forget our science lessons. It is a place that reawakens our awe.

In rediscovering the creatures that can only thrive in an enchanted ecosystem, adults are able to resurrect the faith we had as children— and children are perhaps able to revive the faith that dies so quickly in this media-saturated, innocence-stealing era. We all return to a time when Santa and a giant bunny laden with baskets of sweets were real—but instead of consumerized modern fantasy creatures, we find ourselves in the company of the best and most enduring that the divine magic of human creativity has conjured. Rowling has rescued them from the ruins of lost cultures, giving them new life and validity. By telling us where they have all gone, and that they are alive and well, she gives children permission to believe despite "the facts" and adults permission to stop thinking about whether we "believe" in genetically engineering flying horses and to remember that belief is not an intellectual debate.

Rowling, however, gives us far more than magical creatures: She gives us magic itself, and with it, a validation of longings that begin in childhood and never leave us, although they may be exiled to our sleeping hours. Who hasn't fantasized about having special powers? How gratifying to finally see that bully get his comeuppance; how thrilling to finally be able to fly through the air. And what if imminent doom could be chased away by thoughts of those we love leaping silver and staglike from our minds? What if we knew for a fact that death wasn't annihilation because there were friendly ghosts hanging around to confirm it? Magic may be a science, but unlike our technology, it puts true miracles at its users' fingertips. (In fact, this is why the inhabitants of the magical realm have no need of Muggle science: The forces of nature are theirs to harness with a well-pronounced phrase and the skillful flick of a stick.)

And in Harry Potter's world, like our own, miraculous power encompasses both good and evil, both light and dark. Rowling's magic is not decaffeinated, alcohol-free lite enchantment stripped of any real clout: It is potent wizardry, capable of transformation and destruction, of both saving and taking life. It is a natural superpower that obviously springs from the source of all nature, even though that source is never named and worshipped. And although not a religion, magic—like religion—places the burden of morality on mankind.

For most human beings, morality and our Maker are inextricably intertwined. In striving for goodness, we strive for godliness. In using magic for right and against wrong, the heroes of Rowling's series, despite their inevitable human flaws, are living their faith. And they are living it in a way that we Muggles never can, restricted as we are to a realm where the awesome forces that gave rise to our reality are light-years, and not just a wand-wave, away. Consider Harry and Hermione's Time-Turning in *Harry Potter and the Prisoner of Azkaban* that enables them to save two innocent lives, or the ancient couple in *Harry Potter and the Sorcerer's Stone* who give up immortality for the greater good. Conversely, consider Lord Voldemort's use of horrific Dark Arts to prolong his own existence. Rowling's novels demonstrate how miraculous power, and our relationship with it, determines our fate in this life and beyond. Her stories confirm that although we have free will, we do not exercise it in a vacuum where our actions are devoid of meaning—or eternal consequence. Only in the magical world, your soul cannot just be lost, but actually sucked out of your body.

Many of Harry Potter's fundamentalist critics see morality in absolute terms, with the equivalent of a Dementor's Kiss as punishment for failure to obey God's law. However, most of us live in a reality where our Creator's intent is difficult to discern from ancient and oft-reinterpreted rule books, let alone apply to the ever-more complex questions raised by progress. This is why it is so spiritually refreshing to escape those questions. The heroes of Rowling's tales seem confident of what is right. They prevail (at least, thus far), assuring us that the love of a mother for her child—and what is more magical and divine than that?—is more powerful than the most evil intentions. Harry and Hermione and Ron prevail, assuring us that there is a benevolent force underlying the universe, and that when we align ourselves with it, although bad things may still happen to good people, the good people do ultimately win.

And so, it is obvious—as long as you don't judge a bespectacled boy and his best friends to be *bad* people because they ride broomsticks and break rules—how Rowling's stories grow from the timeless roots of spiritual experience. They validate our deepest yearnings, stimulate our awe, exercise our faith and affirm our perceptions of miraculous power, morality and benevolence. But even this is not enough to explain why our longing for divine magic causes so many of us to long for the next volume in Rowling's series. It does not fully elucidate why we wait years, our enthusiasm undiminished, to share the experiences of the boy with the lightning-bolt scar. What fuels our passion for Harry Potter is more than a desire to flee from a reality that excludes magic, more than the true magic we find in the place to which we flee—it is how these converge in the depth of our identification with Harry himself.

 Like that young wizard, we, as a civilization, have gladly left our former existence behind, but in so doing we have been thrust into a realm where the impossible is possible and where the old rules no longer apply. A place where grave danger (resulting largely from our technological wizardry) is gathering, and where we must rely on our inherent abilities, our courage and our kind hearts to help us figure out what is right and to do it. Yes, there are those who can teach us, who can share wisdom and who can even try to protect us. But since they have inadvertently helped to create the predicament—whether it arose from prophecy or progress—in which we find ourselves, and have failed—whether they serve the Order of the Phoenix or a religious order—to create lasting peace, it is obvious that our elders cannot solve the problems we face.

Thus, we relate profoundly to the Boy Who Lived, because we too live in a time of critical importance—whether we recognize that fact with the naïve perceptivity of a child or the intellectual sophistication of an adult. And because we too must learn to control the wizardry we have inherited if we are to rid the world of evil before it—or our own immature judgment—destroys us. And finally, because our future, like his, depends on developing our relationship with the miraculous power that sustains our reality.

Harry's story, then, is our story, but seen through a very different set of spectacles than the ones we all wear: the poorly coordinated twin lenses of religion, whose clarity is becoming obscured by time, and rationalism, whose focus, as time passes, is clarifying the mysterious into the mundane. When we look through Harry's glasses instead, we see a world that is haunted, yes, but also hauntingly familiar. A world so genuine and enthralling that our attention is wrenched away from the mesmerizing, neon spectacle of our civilization and brought inward, to that which cannot be viewed directly—that which requires belief. And so, we reach for a series of novels that transports us out of our Muggle lives as instantaneously as Portkeys, emancipating us temporarily from our endless summer in the domain of the Dursleys. Because no matter how much the authoritarian voices around us may deny it, we, like Harry, know there is far more to reality than can be seen from our locked window. And we long for that hidden enchantment which goes by so many names.

Of course, if you share Aunt Petunia's view of magic and magical folk, then Rowling's novels are an entirely different experience. For the religious reactionaries, these books open a door that should be kept firmly shut—or even incinerated. But that is because for them, spirituality is synonymous with religion—and most likely, *their* religion.

The irony of the controversy surrounding Harry Potter, then, is that religions are built on a foundation of awe, faith, longing for the miraculous and divine, and a perception of morality and benevolence—the same timeless basis that Rowling's stories use to provide a timely evocation of the spiritual. Her novels do not undermine or attempt to replace traditional beliefs, as critics charge. Their immense appeal arises from the fact that they enable readers to return to the *soul* of those beliefs. The fans and foes of Rowling's series, like Harry and You-Know-Who and like most opposing sides, have more in common than we might care to admit. And, as is so often the case, that which we share generates our conflict, whether it is the power to do great magic or a powerful yearning for the greatest magic of all.

Thankfully, though, devotees and detractors of Harry Potter are not bound to a destiny where only one side can survive! And so, for millions of wistful Muggles around the globe, the pages of Rowling's books are wide open. We enter them by suspending our disbelief in that which we have learned our whole lives is *not* real—and we find something that *is* real. We believe, for 309 or 870 pages, in that which we have never seen, that which cannot be proven, that which is miraculous by its very existence, because *we yearn for just this.*

Yes, on one level the Harry Potter novels succeed, and succeed brilliantly and lucratively and famously, because their author cleverly combines a school-year series, with its best friends and bratty rich kids and mean teachers and juvenile exploits, with an epic fantasy of good and evil, and then fleshes the whole thing out with endless charming detail and utterly engaging characters. But on a deeper level, Rowling's stories capture our minds and hearts because they temporarily fulfill, through fantasy, a universal longing—and an increasingly urgent need—to connect with the hidden magic we know is all around us. In so doing, they bring us home on the wings of our imagination—just as surely as a white owl swooping in an open window.

Sources

Robinson, B. A. "Conservative Christian Boycott of Disney Company." http://www.religioustolerance.org/disney.htm.

Wagner, Rachel. "Bewitching the Box Office: Harry Potter and Religious Controversy." *Journal of Religion and Film.* Vol. 7.2, Oct. 2003.

ELISABETH DEVOS is the author of science fantasy novel *The Seraphim Rising,* as well as short fiction that has appeared in *Talebones* magazine and the anthology *Imagination Fully Dilated.* Her stories explore what happens when mythical, mystical beings collide with the Muggle world of religion and rationalism. Elisabeth grew up near Orlando and earned a B.S. in computer science from the University of Central Florida. She has lived in the Seattle area for over a decade and read her first Harry Potter book while flying diagonally across the country for the umpteenth time.

SARAH ZETTEL

Hermione Granger and the Charge of Sexism

A LOOK, NOT ONLY AT HERMIONE, BUT AT THE BROAD SPECTRUM
OF THE PORTRAYAL OF MEN AND WOMEN IN THE HARRY POTTER
UNIVERSE. A BONA FIDE FEMINIST LOOKS THE *BÊTE NOIRE* IN THE
EYES AND DARES IT TO DO ITS WORST, AND DISCOVERS THAT, AS IS
THE CASE WITH MOST *BÊTES NOIRES*, IT IS SMOKE AND SHADOW.

FIRST, A CONFESSION. I did not want to write this essay. I really didn't. I am a feminist, and the daughter of two feminists, and proud to be so. But writing this essay means making my best effort at intellectual honesty. I would have to go back and read all the Harry Potter books specifically looking for examples of sexism. If I found them, my ability to enjoy the series would be seriously curtailed, and I love the series, deeply and passionately. I love that so many *kids* love the series. Think about it: Millions of kids out there staying up 'til dawn, not because of a movie or a game, but because of a book.

Wow.

But the charge has been made, and it should be answered. So. Here we go. Question: Is the Harry Potter series by J. K. Rowling sexist?

No. Next question?

Okay, perhaps I should elaborate.

First, let me say, I do not consider Harry Potter a feminist series by any stretch of the imagination. The three most powerful figures in the book—one for evil and two for good—are male. As a result, the point of view with which we spend the most time is male. To be a feminist work, a story has to be specifically about issues unique to girls and women and usually has a female protagonist as the main point of view. The Harry Potter books are not intended to be descriptions of the lives of women nor are they prescriptions for how those lives should be lived. Books are necessarily of a finite length and complexity, and an author, even of a fantasy, must choose which ethical questions to present in detail. Rowling chose to make racism the major ethical theme of the Harry Potter books.

However, whenever male and female characters interact within a story the question of gender relations arises, and it has certainly arisen in regards to this series. Since no one should have to stand trial without facing their accusers, for the purpose of this rebuttal I am going to reference three articles that accuse the series of sexism:

"Harry Potter's Girl Trouble: The world of everyone's favorite kid wizard is a place where boys come first," by Christine Schoefer, found at www.salon.com

"'Me! Books! And Cleverness!:' Stereotypical Portrayals in the Harry Potter Series," by Natasha Whitton, found at www.womenwriters.net/summer04/reviews/HarryPotter.htm

"Stepping on the Harry Potter Buzz," by Jane Elliott, found at www.bitchmagazine.com/archives/3_01potter/potter.shtml

All three essays charge that the books are sexist, and they do so in remarkably similar ways. They all charge that the females use their power in ways that make them less appealing than the males, that the females are overall less likeable than the males and that Hermione Granger specifically is less powerful, less self-possessed and less adventurous than the boys.

All three essays also share a primary weakness: They make their charges with no consideration to larger context. The books are dismantled and incidents that fit the argument are rounded up and isolated. Adjectives and quotes are pulled out of the narrative without

reference to point of view, placement within the series or counter-
vailing sentiment on the part of the character or author.

For instance, Whitton's essay only covers the first book, although
it was written when four of the books were available. Consequently, it
does not take into account the growth and maturation undergone by
all the main characters, both female and male. All the juvenile characters have their own individual weaknesses related to background
as well as age. To have them see and understand the complexities of
the world perfectly from the get-go would not only be unrealistic, it
would be astoundingly bad storytelling. In a good *modern* novel no
character, male or female, is perfect. In fact, Rowling is taking a serious risk by playing up many of her characters' flaws as they age, and
in making them in some ways less likeable and charming than they
were in the beginning.

Much is made, in all the articles, of the adjectives used to describe
the women in the books. Of particular concern is the paragraph describing the guests at the Leaky Cauldron in *Harry Potter and the
Prisoner of Azkaban*. The phrase Whitton takes for examination is
"funny little witches." In her article, however, the sentence goes unfinished. The whole phrase is "funny little witches from the country
up for a bit of shopping," which, if taken in its complete form, says
less that they are funny and little because they're witches than because they're bumpkins.

It is Schoefer, however, who makes the clearest misinterpretation
by removing quotes from context. In her essay, she makes great objection to the assessment of Ginny in *Harry Potter and the Chamber
of Secrets*. Schoefer writes:

> Ron's younger sister, Ginny, another girl student at Hogwarts...fares
> even worse than Hermione. "Stupid little Ginny" unwittingly be-
> comes the tool of evil when she takes to writing in a magical diary. For
> months and months, "the foolish little brat" confides "all her pitiful
> worries and woes" ("How she didn't think famous good great Harry
> Potter would 'ever' like her") to these pages. We are told how boring it
> is to listen to "the silly little troubles of an eleven-year-old girl."

If one of the protagonists, or the omniscient narrator, had uttered the quotes Schoefer pulls out in that paragraph, I would be standing shoulder-to-shoulder with her regarding sexism in the books. However, Schoefer fails to mention the most vital fact about this spate of derision: It is the villain, Lord Voldemort, who is speaking here. The adult "authority" in the book who finds Ginny ridiculous is a mass murderer known for his cold, calculated seduction and manipulation of anybody who might help him get his way. Of course Voldemort finds Ginny pathetic! He finds anybody who exhibits human emotion pathetic.

Context is vital in literary analysis, and nowhere more than here. We are not asked or expected to admire Lord Voldemort. While in later books, such as *Harry Potter and the Half-Blood Prince*, we are given background that makes him more fully fleshed as a character, Voldemort is never presented as in any way fair or admirable. So, when he sneers at a character, we as readers are not being told to take his statements as an accurate assessment of that character's worth. We are being shown that such an attitude is at the least seriously flawed.

To put Ginny even more firmly in her own context, she, like the other characters, grows up during the course of the books. By *Harry Potter and the Order of the Phoenix*, she proves to be highly intelligent, not to mention adept at athletics, academics and magic. She is so good at magic, in fact, that in *Half-Blood Prince*, Professor Slughorn includes her in his parties even though she has no powerful connections. Unlike Harry, but much like Hermione, she gets into "the Slug Club" on raw magical talent.

She actively battles evil and is not afraid of taking risks or following them through. Ultimately, she also finds success in love by accepting the advice of her good friend Hermione and taking the time to just be herself.

Come to that, while we're talking about the Weasleys, you'll notice something else about them. As the stories progress, it's not Ginny who's the weak link in the family. It's authority-loving Percy, her older brother. Male Percy's the true sycophant, up to the point where he is willing to desert his family out of blind adherence to authority.

What seems to be the major argument of sexism in the books for both Elliott and Schoefer is that the authority of the women and girls is not "appealing." Elliott's main objection seems to be the series' tone when showing its female characters. She writes: "It's this negative cast that Hermione's defenders keep missing....Hermione, Professor McGonagall and even Ron's mother, Mrs. Weasley, are indisputably powerful, but their power is also associated with a shrill recital of rules and codes of behavior." Later, she says, "But for female characters, even 'good' authority appears only in the shrill, limiting rule-bound variety. Men make people free and safe in these books, while women merely tell them what to do." Elliott also says, "My complaint is not that the books are about a boy...but that the female characters are so stereotypically negative: the bossy, goody-goody girl; the stern spinster teacher; the mother whose only skill is self-sacrifice...."

According to Elliott and Schoefer, the problem (to borrow from a very different American writer, namely Arthur Miller) is that the females are not well liked. They are certainly not well liked by the boys who cannot, or will not, see the consequences of their own actions.

Here again, if that was all we were being shown, I would be in complete agreement. But it isn't. I'm going to save the analysis of Hermione for the end, but let's look at the other specific charges now:

"The stern spinster teacher." I'm assuming we're talking about Minerva McGonagall here. Okay, stern's a fair charge: McGonagall is strict, and is consistently portrayed as so. She runs a tough class and she does not favor the students of her own house. This might make her hard to like in a friendly way, but she's also fair, as opposed to the increasingly evil and hated Snape, who blatantly favors students from his own house.

Whether or not the boys (with their flawed vision) like McGonagall, the author shows that she is a better teacher than a number of her male counterparts, and expert at a more complex magic in addition to being the head of a house esteemed for its courage and boldness. Transfiguration, her class, is shown to be a difficult and dangerous subject. Without discipline and concentration it could seriously harm the students. Everyone is anxious to pass Professor Mc-

Gonagall's Transfiguration class because it is a vital subject for them, while none of them want to continue with friendly, loveable Hagrid's Care of Magical Creatures class. As an aside, you'll note that during these lessons they think wistfully of the female teacher Grubbly-Plank.

This is not to say that McGonagall is not flawed. Like many people at the school, she has a pronounced weakness for sports, and bends the rules to allow Harry to play Quidditch in his first year with his own broom. Come to that, she bends them again, more severely and on her own authority, to allow Hermione use of a restricted magical artifact so Hermione can fully pursue her academic ambitions. These facts are overlooked in the consistent charge that the female authority figures adhere mindlessly to the rules and are no fun at all.

Also to be considered: McGonagall is, at the beginning, trusted with the secret of Harry's whereabouts and protection. This means it is expected that if she were caught and tortured, she would be strong and brave enough to keep her silence. She is also second in command at Hogwarts. Taken in itself, this can be seen as a position of subjugation, but when looked at within the context of the narrative, this is not a comfortable or easy place to be. Dumbledore knows the dangers that face the school, and that he might fail, or be absent at a critical moment, so it is Minerva McGonagall he trusts to watch his back, and take care of the school and the students in the face of evil that might destroy them. This is not a portrayal of female weakness.

"Spinster" is a more complex charge. As near as I can tell, none of the Hogwarts teachers, male or female, are married, let alone have kids. The place is a positive academic monastery. For the life of me I don't know why Rowling chose to make it this way; perhaps it's that pesky finite length problem again. It is, however, even-handed. There are no professors' husbands, but there are no professors' wives either.

Elliott's charges continue with "The mother whose only skill is self-sacrifice." Here I assume she's talking about Lily Potter née Evans. Lily casts the most powerful spell in the series. It is her action that defeats the curse that no one can defeat, cast by the most evil wizard ever, and it costs her her life. While that's hardly weak, or foolish, I can see the charge of sexism really sticking here. Mother-sacrificing-all-for-child is a literary cliché that goes back a long, long way, and it annoyed me as a kid. I will freely admit that, from my personal point of view, it annoys me rather less since I've become a mother myself. Here once more, though, Schoefer ignores the narrative context in which Lily and all the other mothers are placed as the series unfolds.

As we go through the series, we learn more and more about Lily Evans. According to Slughorn, who is not an admirable character but has an eye for talent, she was a brilliant student. While they were at school, it was James who was a prat, and Lily who refused to be taken in by his looks or impressed by his athletic skills. After school, Lily was a member of the original Order of the Phoenix when Voldemort first came to power. This means after she had married James and while she was pregnant with Harry, she was still actively fighting a deadly enemy who had no compunction about killing women and children. She did not go into hiding because she had become a mother. Rather, by her activities in the resistance, she made herself a target. That's the point that raises Lily above a simple cliché. If she'd hidden "just" because she was going to have a child, I'd accept that she was a pure stereotypical mother figure, but she stayed in the fight, even while she had an infant. I'm not sure I'd have that kind of dedication or nerve.

Lily is, of course, not the only mother in the series. Another mother we get a good look at is Narcissa Malfoy. From what we've seen so far, she has chosen the side of evil just as freely and as actively as her husband. It would not be unreasonable to speculate that she married Lucius because he shared views she had before the marriage. I'd suggest she's the antithesis of Lily Potter, particularly when it comes to what happens when their children are in danger. Lily faced the danger on her own and paid the price herself.

Narcissa begs someone else, and a male at that, to sacrifice himself for her child while she stays relatively safe at home. By showing us Narcissa Rowling shows us, again, that what makes women and girls good or strong is not their association (or lack thereof) with men, but their own choices and actions.

In contrast to this active seeking of evil, we have Merope, Lord Voldemort's mother. What's interesting here is the part she and her relationships take in the continuing themes of race and class. Lily, the lower class, mixed-"race" woman, is an excellent student from a sound family, capable of great courage and great love. Merope, like Narcissa, is the pure-blood member of the hereditary nobility and, also like Narcissa, is broken by her family circumstances and probably beyond repair. But where Narcissa walks into deliberate evil, Merope is a victim of abuse who can only fall in love with someone who scorns her. Rowling's whole segment regarding Merope was, in fact, a shudderingly realistic portrayal of domestic abuse and its consequences.

I've got to pause here for a moment and cheer this attention to detail. It is unusual in a fantasy novel for mothers to each have their own unique story that makes them fully fledged people, not just mothers. We even get that a bit with Petunia Dursley. If there are blatant caricatures in the book, they are the Dursleys. But the only one of the Dursleys who's even vaguely nuanced is Aunt Petunia. She is the one who in the end understands that to throw Harry out of the house is to condemn him to death, and she is the one unwilling to do that. Even in the middle of the most absurd section of the series, it is the female in the scene who clearly sees the consequences and acts on that knowledge.

The mother with whom we spend the most time is, of course, Molly Weasley. She's a powerful witch in her own right. Even Dumbledore is impressed by her abilities. On top of this, she's successfully raising seven kids on a tight budget. Honestly, the woman should get a medal. And, like Lily, she was an active participant in the original Order of the Phoenix, while she had five young children to look out for. Charlie, Bill, Percy and the twins, because they are all older than Harry, must have been born while Voldemort still held power.

But she's still a stickler for discipline, and this negates her other qualities in Elliott's analysis. Here again, I have to disagree. Codes of behavior are most certainly not all Molly brings to the book. Harry not only needs a father figure, he needs a mother figure, and he's got one in Mrs. Weasley, who welcomes him into her home and family and offers him all the security, protection and guidance she's got to give. Yes, she's a big one for the rules and for not taking chances. Again, within context, this makes a great deal of sense. She lived through Voldemort's reign. She knows he will kill children, and she knows he's out there right now. Added to that, she's got to ride herd on seven magical kids. If she doesn't take a strict line, they're going to get themselves killed because they've turned each other into mosquitoes or blown each other up. Her adherence to caution and rules is not born of timidity, blindness or some uniquely female failing, but because she can see the consequences and they are dire. Do the boys like it? No. Teenage boys never like rules or, at least, constantly say they do not. But those same teenage boys cannot see those consequences. If they could, they would be in far fewer scrapes and might even live longer, a fact that the author makes plain during the course of the narrative.

Does Molly Weasley continue to fight Lord Voldemort and support the fight against him with seven kids and full knowledge of what it might mean? Yes. This is the strength shared by the adult women in the Harry Potter series. Clear-eyed and mindful of the consequences to themselves and others, they move forward.

Another possible charge for the appearance of sexism in the books might be that Molly, our most positive mother, is in a highly traditional relationship. Mr. Weasley goes out and works, and Mrs. Weasley stays home and looks after their seven children. This raises a problem any modern female author faces. How do you portray a traditionally structured family? You cannot pretend they don't exist. No one will believe you. Okay, this is a fantasy, so one could do a lot with magic as it impacts family structure, if one wanted to, but to erase the nuclear family structure and make it believable would take up a whole lot of wordage, something that is in short supply in a young adult novel. Alternately, you can choose not to focus on traditional families, but as we are dealing with children, families are very important and cannot be left out of the stories.

I'm going to go out on a limb here. I've thought a lot about this one, as a feminist, and as an author. How *should* traditional roles be portrayed? In fantasy literature there is a school of thought that holds that women must be treated precisely like men. Only the traditional male sphere of power and means of wielding power count. If a woman is shown in a traditionally female role, then she must be being shown as inferior.

After a lot of thought, and some real-life stabs at those traditional roles, I've come to firmly disagree with this idea. For an author to show that only traditional male power and place matter is to discount and belittle the hard and complex lives of our peers and our ancestresses. The best way to do it is what Rowling does—to show the traditional role as one possibility among many, and to show it as both negative and positive according to the choices of the person playing the role. Beyond their roles as mothers and wives, women are active in government and law enforcement. Women own their own businesses. Women teach, and are and have been headmistresses of magical schools. Hermione's from a solid, supportive, two-income family. The girls at Hogwarts are educated in complete equality with the boys, and there is no bar to their joining in athletics, or even coaching and captaining the teams. The only difference between the treatment of the genders at the school is that the girl's dormitory is booby-trapped to prevent the boys from entering, but the girls can freely enter the boys'. You will notice, however, that Hermione's assessment of this single difference in treatment is that it is "old-fashioned."

Which brings us finally and firmly around to Hermione Granger.

The complaints made against Hermione's portrayal in these three articles, and in others, are wide-ranging and manifold. One such criticism is about how she gets her buck teeth fixed in time for the Yule ball. The complaint is that Hermione needs to be physically transformed when the boys don't. Yes, Hermione changes her looks both there and by the judicious application of magical hair gel later, but you'll notice something important: Hermione herself changes her looks. Nobody else changes her. She changes what she wants on her own, in her own way and of her own choosing. No boy or man tells her she needs to dress up, or fix her teeth. No one helps her. Turns out she knows full well how to make herself attractive, she just doesn't like to bother. This is not a Cinderella story where a higher power must make a girl worthy of her prince: This is deliberate choice and action.

It should also be noted that almost the first thing Rowling says from Harry's point of view is that the only thing *he* likes about his appearance is his scar. Ron also is concerned about his appearance and ashamed of his old-fashioned dress robes.

Another complaint is that Hermione cries. You know what? So do I. I've cried when I've lost contracts. Once I even cried over a particularly bad critiquing session with my writer's group. God knows I cried in high school when picked on for my beliefs, looks or actions. I've cried in public, and I've cried in the ladies room. Damned embarrassing. Makes you cry harder.

Which leads us to the famous troll incident, where Hermione balks and needs rescuing. Leaving aside the fact that all three of the heroes at various times need rescuing, there's a piece of context for this incident that gets left out of many of the analyses of it: Hermione is in trouble not because she was reduced to tears, but because the males around her made a series of mistakes. The male Professor Quirrell released the troll because he was possessed by the male Lord Voldemort. Ron's insults broke down Hermione's self-confidence causing her to flee. Ron and Harry's ill-informed act of locking the bathroom door put Hermione in more jeopardy than the troll did. It was because of a group of males—including the hero—that Hermione was suddenly in a room with a dangerous monster, all alone, with no escape route.

She also balks, and badly, during the final adventure in *Harry Potter and the Sorcerer's Stone*; she forgets that as a witch she can conjure the fire needed to defeat the Devil's Snare and, later, makes a self-deprecatory speech to Harry about how he is the true hero and her ability is only books and cleverness.

Yes, Hermione's got a classic cliché embedded in her character there. She lacks self-esteem, and it gets in her way, especially in the early books. Again, if Hermione only existed to be rescued and show the boy's heroism, I would agree that she is a subjugated figure and an example of sexism. But that's not all she is. She is a friend and an advisor. She is able to protect and defend, and think ahead when the boys are going along blindly. For instance, it's Hermione who works out how to make sure nobody snitches on the Dumbledore's Army meetings. She is sensible when the boys are foolish.

This is a trait which more than any other brings her in for some heat, both inside the books, and outside.

Of Hermione's cautionary role, Elliott says, "We've all seen this kind of character before—the one who's always shrieking 'Be careful!' or 'This is insane!' at the hero while he's busy doing something admirable and risky."

I agree. The lone, smart, disagreeable girl in the crowd of boys is a cliché. She is all over children's stories these days, especially children's television. I know this firsthand; I am compelled to watch a lot of children's TV with my son. There is, however, a big difference between Hermione and most of these others. In most children's tales, that lone, smart girl has to be put in her place. She's rude, and must be taught politeness, or she acts like she's smarter than others when she really isn't and must be shown the error of her ways. Alternately, she must be taught to listen to other people's ideas. Now THAT'S real sexism. If one asked the writers of these little episodes, they'd surely say "Look, we're not sexist, because we're saying it's okay for a girl to be really smart." No, they're saying it's okay as long as the girl doesn't act TOO smart, or get uppity. It's as bad as the old Katharine Hepburn movies where Kate's smart, and successful, and always, always has to be shown that it means nothing if she so much as verbally wounds Spencer Tracy or, Heaven forbid, divorces Cary Grant because he's a drunk.

94

That is most definitely not, however, the portrait of a smart girl in Rowling's world. Hermione doesn't just think she's right most of the time; she *is* right most of the time. If the boys get grumpy about it, it's less because she's rude, or wrong, than because *they're* wrong, and it is in human nature not to like to be shown up as having made a mistake, especially an important one. This is even more in the nature of teenagers than adults. Hermione sometimes looks foolish to her friends and classmates, but she is seldom wrong, and the other kids, who accept the prevailing wisdom and status quo, don't like her for it.

It is important to see, however, that the disdain comes from the other characters, not from the author. If the author disdained and disrespected her character's vigilance and tactics, Hermione would fail. She would apologize and change her mind, not just her tactics. She would be untrustworthy and belittled. She's not. At the end of every adventure and encounter, Hermione is shown to have been in the right, and she stuck with it, whether the boys liked it or not. Let me say that again. *She stuck with it, whether the boys liked it or not.* The boys scold, quarrel and pick on her fairly constantly. Despite this, Hermione does nothing, ever, just because the boys would like her better for it. She does what she does because her own judgment tells her it is right. Hermione, and Ginny with her, are overlooked and misunderstood by the boys, but not by the author. This is the crucial point. Taken in context, Rowling shows boys' treatment of the girls to be, in turns, callous, foolish or, in the particular case of ignoring Hermione's advice, dangerous.

Schoefer's essay focuses on the fact that she believes Hermione to be fighting for the boy's good opinion. Schoefer writes: "She struggles so hard to get Harry and Ron's approval and respect, in spite of the boys' constant teasing and rejection."

I strongly disagree. It's not that Hermione doesn't care what Ron and Harry think of her, it's that she doesn't let their opinions get in the way of doing what she knows to be right. You see, aside from attention to context, here's what's really missing from all three of these essays:

Harry Potter may not be a feminist series, but Hermione Granger is a feminist.

Oh yes, she is.

Hermione publicly and unashamedly pursues the course she knows to be right, even when it costs her her friends or the regard of male authority figures. She is not deterred by the prevailing opinion of society. If she is not initially effective, she tries other methods to achieve her right ends. She is, in the main, highly confident in her own understanding, and that confidence frequently pays off. She forcefully argues her points and does not back down when ignored. She brings every weapon she's got to bear into her particular fight, and she succeeds, even if it takes a while. She is also conscious that the boys have some blinders when it comes to the abilities of girls, and she does not take this lightly. In *Half-Blood Prince*, it's Hermione, true to form, who works out that "Prince" might be a woman's surname rather than a man's title. The boys sneer at the notion. Also as usual, Hermione ignores their derision and goes forward on her own path, because she's certain she might be right, and this is important, so she will pursue it. Hermione never rests on previous opinions and preconceptions. She analyzes her situation rigorously. She follows authority when she sees it being exerted fairly, not just forcefully, and never allows a simple order from an authority figure, male or female, to override her own good judgment. Hermione makes the first real, open challenge to Dolores Umbridge. Hermione is the one who refuses to cower and be silent when threatened by Rita Skeeter's pen.

Then there's the contrast to Ron. Ron is held up as the more easily likeable of the two. So I thought, until I went back and read the series again. If Hermione can be a bossy goody-two-shoes, Ron can be a positive git. Ron's insulting, quick to judge, quick to fight, skives off classwork constantly and needs Hermione to get him through. He's also jealous, possessive and ashamed of his relative poverty. In *Chamber of Secrets*, the only thing Ron does is break his own wand, creating the plot device that overcomes Professor Lockhart in the end. Hermione's annoying traits tend to rescue any given situation. Ron's tend to make them worse. Yes, Hermione needs to be rescued in the middle of *Sorcerer's Stone*, but at the climax of *Prisoner of Azkaban*, Ron is nowhere to be found and it is only with Hermione's help that Harry succeeds.

Hermione, with her superior judgment and clarity of perception, never ceases to be a gadfly. Hermione's predecessor is less those fantasy heroines Dorothy Gale and Lucy Pevensie, and more the cursed Greek prophetess Cassandra. Because of this, Rowling shows Hermione getting what prophets and gadflies get: disdain.

Is it a mistake on the part of the author to show Hermione being picked on for her adherence to her own interpretation of the rules and her insistence on seeing the consequences of action? I don't think so. These books are not science fiction set in an idealized future. They are also not set in a completely imagined world where the author is free to make up all the rules of social interaction. They are set, relatively speaking, in the here and now. Hermione is from the world of the late twentieth/early twenty-first century. She grew up under its social pressures, the good ones and the bad ones. The results of these social pressures include caring about one's looks, caring about achievement, self-esteem issues of all varieties and differences in communication styles.

No, Hermione is not portrayed exactly like the boys in the book, but the boys aren't portrayed as exactly like each other either. As another YA author Madeline L'Engle put it so eloquently so many years ago, "Alike and equal are not the same thing." It would be ludicrous for Rowling to write Hermione as if social and peer pressures neither existed nor mattered. They do exist. They do matter, and the girls who are growing up reading these books deal with them every day, as does Hermione.

So in fact, do Schoefer and Elliott.

Schoefer writes: "Bringing up my objections has earned me other parents' resentment—they regard me as a heavy-handed feminist with no sense of fun who is trying to spoil a bit of magic they had discovered."

Elliott writes: ". . . feminists and other critical thinkers often find ourselves cast in real-life versions of Hermione's killjoy role."

Come to that, I got a treatment similar to Hermione's and Schoefer and Elliott's. Back in my blue-collar suburb, I was the only outspoken feminist in my various schools. I was also considered ugly, unpopular and thought to have a problem keeping my mouth shut. There was, in fact, a gym teacher who went around telling his classes, "None of you girls grow up to be feminists, or you'll end up like Sarah Zettel."

Where was Hermione when I was growing up? I could have used her.

Another point about Hermione: Yes, she harps on rules and the possibility of expulsion more than the boys. She's also more concerned about her academics. This makes perfect sense in terms of character, not because she's a girl, but because she's from a non-magical family. Whitton actually brings up this question. Of Hermione, she says, "She has already informed Harry and Ron that she has read all of the books for the term and done extensive additional research to prove herself worthy of a Hogwarts education, whether because she is a girl or part-Muggle is not entirely clear."

If Hermione fails Hogwarts, she's sunk. She can't exactly go back home and become a dentist. Unlike Ron, she's got no family to help her. Unlike Harry, she has no fame. She is absolutely on her own, and it is by her own merits and actions she must make good. Her position, therefore, is more precarious than that of either of the boys, and she shows by her actions she is aware of this.

Yet, despite all that, she is still perfectly willing and able to set fire to a professor's robes if she thinks he's cheating during a Quidditch game, or openly confront the Ministry of Magic stooge who has the power to torture and expel her, in that order.

I do not say that all the portrayals of women in the Harry Potter series are nuanced or fair. Madam Pince the librarian goes irrational when she thinks a student has written in a book. But then, Filch the caretaker wants the students whipped and chained for littering. The Fat Lady has no name of her own, and drinks too much at Christmas. But then, Peeves, the most persistent and obnoxious spirit in the castle, is male.

98

So's the wizard who tried to teach trolls ballet, and the one who tried to invent the cheese cauldron. Trelawney is a fraud who drinks too much and doesn't recognize her own power when it comes on her. Dudley is a ludicrous bully. His father is a ludicrous bully. Draco Malfoy's a racist and an inch away from being a murderer. This balance matters with regards to the charge of sexism. If only the females were shown to be flawed, then the charge of sexism would be serious and real, but that would also be the case if only the males were shown to be flawed. The people in Rowling's books come in all shapes, sizes and modes of behavior, just like people in the real world. Critics deride the girls at Hogwarts because they are shown to giggle and shriek and generally make a lot of noise. Some real, live girls do giggle and shriek. Some are quiet and serious. Some like pink and ruffles. Some like athletics and blue jeans. We see them all at Hogwarts. I reject the notion that we must tell girls that the only way to be valid human beings is to turn themselves into boys. I also reject the notion that authors must portray them that way. There are girls at Hogwarts who are vain and ridiculous. There are girls who are bookish and studious, or shy and uncertain. There are girls who are geeks. In Rowling's world, they are all okay, no matter what their peers think of them. They all can, and do, choose to stand up for what's right and lay their own lives on the line if need be. What Rowling ultimately shows in these books is that no matter who you are, you can be yourself and still be a worthy person.

I cannot think of a better message for the girls and young women of the world.

SARAH ZETTEL was born in Sacramento, California. Since then she has lived in ten cities, four states, two countries and become an author of a dozen science fiction and fantasy books, a host of short stories and novellas, as well as a handful of essays about the pop culture in which she finds herself immersed. She lives in Michigan with her husband Tim, son Alexander and cat Buffy the Vermin Slayer. When not writing, she drinks tea, gardens, practices tai chi and plays the fiddle, but not all at once.

Neville Longbottom: The Hero with a Thousand Faces

As we have learned, there was some doubt as to whether the person destined to oppose Lord Voldemort was Harry Potter or Neville Longbottom. Martha Wells' essay points out just how close to the Campbellian pattern the much-abused and woefully ordinary Neville really is.

Neville Longbottom is my hero. Yes, I know Harry is the main character and the hero of the series, and the focus of the book-universe, and the only one who can save us, and all that. And I like Harry, I really do. But Neville's my man.

This seems to be true for a lot of fans, who from the beginning hoped that Neville would have a bigger role in the series, simply because Neville is very easy not only to sympathize with, but to identify with as well. Neville's life sucks beyond the telling of it, and yet he perseveres. Not that he has much choice. He has a lot more in common with most of us in the audience, in that respect, than someone like Harry, who regularly affects the circumstances of his own life. But I also think that Neville is really a hero, in his own corner of the Harry Potter universe.

Despite the general ordinariness of Neville's existence in the first two books, fans had long speculated that Neville was destined for something greater: that he would be instrumental somehow in the final battle against Voldemort or prove to be just as badass a wizard as Harry. I don't think this was just wishful thinking, a side effect of identifying with a sympathetic character, though Neville is an easy kid to feel drawn to. His life is pretty normal. He's a little overweight. He's intelligent, and he does well when he gets good instruction, but he's not brilliant, he's not a natural at anything except working with magical plants. He has low self-esteem—and with his family, who can blame him?

But I think that to a large extent readers were picking up on, both consciously and subconsciously, the elements of Neville's character that reflect the typical trappings of the hero in Western culture. And in many ways, Neville has continued to follow the typical hero model as the series has progressed.

Neville's life in *Harry Potter and the Sorcerer's Stone* is not much of a grand adventure, which is pretty incredible when you think about it. The kid has magical powers and he goes to a magical school for wizards, with flying broomsticks and magic candy and talking portraits. Neville's life should be an adventure, even if the wizarding life, like our own, obviously has its ups and downs. But Neville's life seems to be mostly just downs.

School can be brutal for kids in real life. But while Neville doesn't have to worry about drug dealers and school shootings (though Fred and George do get a little scary occasionally with the joke candies that enlarge people's tongues and so on), he does have to worry about monsters and Voldemort and whichever psycho nutjob is currently masquerading as the new Defense Against the Dark Arts teacher. (I personally love the fact that up until Snape took it over in *Harry Potter and the Half-Blood Prince,* the only decent teacher of that class turned out to be a werewolf. And not just a cute Disney human-in-wolf-form, but a real werewolf who has no control over it and might end up eating you by mistake.) So with all this to contend with, you would think that Neville's life would involve a lot of adventure, high and low. Except it didn't, at least not at first.

In *Sorcerer's Stone,* we find out poor Neville was thought to be "all-

102

Muggle," or a Squib, until he was eight. Neville's Great Uncle Algie kept trying to startle Neville into performing magic, and Neville mentions in particular the time Great Uncle Algie dropped him off Blackpool Pier and he nearly drowned. This unusual parenting technique finally bore fruit when Great Uncle Algie dangled Neville out of a second-story window by the ankles, and then accidentally let go. Neville's incipient magical talent allowed him to bounce to safety instead of being killed instantly. It's mentioned later in the book that Neville is afraid of flying, and has difficulty making his broomstick work. Gosh, I wonder where he could have gotten that fear of heights? Any thoughts, Great Uncle Algie?

Neville's grandmother sends Howlers, those magical mail bombs that, when you open them, shriek at you like a demented shrieking thing. In public, at breakfast, in front of all the other students. Personally, I'd chew my own arm off to get away from a parent or guardian who thought it was a good idea to publicly humiliate a basically well-behaved kid whose only crime is being a little absent-minded and clumsy. Newsflash to Grandma: *Step off. He'll grow out of it. Too bad you won't ever grow out of what's wrong with you.* I'd even go to Hogwarts to get away from her, where Voldemort is trying to kill the kid in the next bed over, my favorite teacher may accidentally eat me and there's a good chance of getting mauled in Care of Magical Creatures.

Hogwarts has its own share of bullies, but the bullying from Draco and the other Slytherins seem almost impersonal. Draco's group does that to a lot of people, though Ron often gets the worse end of that stick. (The "Weasley Is Our King" scene springs to mind. Ouch.) I find the bullying Neville gets from his grandmother to be worse. Emotional abuse from people who are supposed to be on your side is always more detrimental than impersonal attacks from the school's designated bullies. Professor Snape also torments Neville in Potions, but then Snape does this to Harry, Ron and apparently most of the other students in his classes. And while Snape's classroom style isn't particularly good, to put it mildly, he has a point. Potions are dangerous, and you can kill yourself and others with them. Even meticulous Hermione comes to grief with her Polyjuice Potion in *Harry*

Potter and the Chamber of Secrets. Potions seem to be something that, if you can't get them right every time, you really shouldn't be messing with them at all.

Neville's early life sets him up as something of a Cinderella figure, paralleling Harry's miserable treatment at the hands of the Dursleys. Again, it's not unreasonable for readers steeped in the heroic and adventure traditions of Western literature to pick up on this and expect that Neville will be shown to have hidden talents or a mysterious destiny as well. But Neville also fits comparative mythologist Joseph Campbell's universal hero pattern, which just reinforces the feeling that the character is meant for more.

Campbell's hero arc includes the following aspects:

- ◆ a miraculous origin or birth
- ◆ a call to adventure
- ◆ trials and challenges in which the hero confronts and defeats his or her inner demons
- ◆ a mentor or spiritual guide that aids the hero in these confrontations
- ◆ descent into the underworld or equivalent, where the hero faces an ultimate nemesis
- ◆ rebirth and resurrection, after which the hero returns to his or her people with the gift of knowledge

Neville's initial "Squibdom," his torture by Uncle Algie and the tragedy surrounding his parents that is revealed in *Harry Potter and the Goblet of Fire* can be seen as fulfilling the "miraculous origin or birth" requirement. And Neville's admission to Hogwarts certainly qualifies as a "call to adventure," especially when he, against his and everyone else's expectations, is sorted into Gryffindor, the Hogwarts House commonly associated with heroic deeds.

Neville goes through trials and challenges and faces and confronts inner demons pretty much constantly, with a gutsiness-in-spite-of-a-wholly-justified-terror that is Neville's hallmark. He's afraid of a lot of things, often justifiably so, and yet he's forced to confront many of them every day of his life. Even if a reader doesn't pick up on this as a pattern consistent with the hero archetype, it's damn hard not to sympathize. Or to hope that it presages greater things.

I felt one of Neville's greatest acts of courage came in *Harry Potter and the Prisoner of Azkaban*, when he admitted that he was the one who wrote down the Gryffindor passwords and then lost them, compromising the security of their dormitory. It's this courage in taking responsibility for his actions, facing potential humiliation, and loss of friendship and what little status he had managed to achieve, as well as being willing to admit that he has put his friends in danger through carelessness, that makes Neville stand out. This isn't an example of magical adventure heroics; it's an example of real-life, everyday, non-sexy heroics from which any reader could benefit. Despite his mistakes, Neville is a true, solid friend. It's one of Neville's best qualities that his support for Harry never wavers no matter what rumors fly or what the *Daily Prophet* says.

And speaking of Harry: a hero also needs a spiritual guide, and while Dumbledore fulfills this function for Harry, we also see Harry to some extent fulfilling this function for Neville. Even though he gets annoyed with Neville at times, Harry is mostly supportive of him, telling him in *Sorcerer's Stone* that he's "worth twelve of Malfoy." And Neville does seem to want to emulate Harry.

Before *Harry Potter and the Order of the Phoenix*, some fans speculated that Neville would play a low-key but important role in the war against Voldemort, probably involving his ability to work so well with magical plants. He would survive the war and come out a stronger individual. But Neville goes through some important changes in *Order of the Phoenix* that take him further down the hero's path, suggesting that he may play an even more essential part in the series' conclusion than even his most devoted fans had guessed.

It's first revealed in *Goblet of Fire* why Neville is so distressed by the subject of patients who are in St. Mungo's because of magical damage to their brains. His parents were members of the Order of the Phoenix, and were tortured with the Cruciatus Curse until they were driven insane. This is obviously one of Neville's inner demons. In *Order of the Phoenix*, Neville is willing to attack Draco for an offhand remark not even aimed at him: "[A]s for Potter...my father says it's a matter of time before the Ministry has him carted off to St. Mungo's. . . . [A]pparently they've got a special ward for people whose brains have been addled by magic."

We see how Neville faces this demon when Harry, Ron and Hermione run into him in the St. Mungo's Incurable Ward, where he and his grandmother are visiting his parents. The humor in Neville's characterization suddenly seems cruel (well, it always seemed a little cruel to me) when we see the pathos of his parents: how his mother gives him the gum wrapper, a sign that she possibly does remember him. Neville is afraid the others will laugh at her, but to his credit, Harry ". . . did not think he'd ever found anything less funny in his life."

Scenes like this contribute to the feeling that Neville is destined for something better than simply a further demonstration of Voldemort's abuse of power. Something, it seems certain, will happen to him to mitigate this tragedy and give it greater meaning.

The "Christmas on the Closed Ward" chapter in *Order of the Phoenix* also sets the scene for Neville's defeat—or at least struggle against—another of his demons: the first time we see Neville admit aloud that he isn't happy with the way his grandmother is continually pointing out to apparently everyone she knows, as well as random strangers on the street, that Neville doesn't have the kind of talent his father had. (Okay, fine, that's not exactly how he puts it, but seriously, I can't stand that woman. Even Uncle Algie, who gives Neville a highly rare plant as an acknowledgement of his growing skill in Herbology, looks more supportive, and this is taking into account the Blackpool Pier incident.)

You could make the case that Neville actually completes his hero's journey in *Order of the Phoenix*. It's Neville's extracurricular lessons in Defense Against the Dark Arts with Harry and the other students in Dumbledore's Army that cause him to "improve beyond all recognition" in his ability to use defensive magic. And in the end Neville insists on going to the Ministry with the others when Harry wants to try to rescue Sirius, though Harry tries to dissuade him. Neville replies: "We were all in the DA together. . . . It was all supposed to be about fighting You-Know-Who, wasn't it? And this is the first chance we've had to do something real—or was that all just a game or something?" This shows us just how far Neville has come since his introduction in *Sorcerer's Stone*.

At the Ministry, it's Neville who fights at Harry's side after Ron and Hermione are incapacitated. Neville even faces the Cruciatus Curse at the hands of Bellatrix Lestrange, the witch who helped torture his parents. The climax of the hero's story is his descent into the underworld to confront his ultimate nemesis, and the battle in the Ministry with the Death Eaters, in particular the confrontation with Bellatrix, fits this requirement well.

It's after this battle that Dumbledore reveals that Neville also fits the prophecy that sealed Harry's destiny—that but for a twist of fate, Neville could very well have been in Harry's position now, as the Boy Who Lived, the boy who is destined to destroy or be destroyed by Voldemort. In *Half-Blood Prince*, Dumbledore adds that it was only Voldemort's belief in the prophecy, and Voldemort's assumption that it was Harry who the prophecy described, that distinguished between them.

On the one hand, this is a powerful statement about the consequences of our choices and the nature of prophecy, and Neville's role may simply be to act as Harry's foil, a human reminder that Harry's status as chosen was neither inevitable nor earned. But after the revelations in *Order of the Phoenix*, I'm personally a little afraid it indicated that Neville will heroically die in the last book, perhaps taking Harry's place.

Imagine if Neville's life had been the focus of the prophecy, instead. Harry would have still been invited to go to Hogwarts because of who his parents were, and still had the chance to live in the wizarding world rather than with the Dursleys. In fact, he might have grown up with his mother and father both still alive, and Uncle Sirius visiting at holidays. He might not have been a Parseltongue, or quite as talented with magic, but he would have still been good at Quidditch, still had friends, still had the chance to have adventures. What he wouldn't have had is the constant scrutiny and attention that comes from being the Boy Who Lived. I don't think he would have balked at giving that up. Harry also would have avoided having access to Voldemort's thoughts, and the crushing responsibility of being the one prophesied to kill Voldemort. Not having to wake up every morning to that destiny probably wouldn't be a bad thing.

But if Neville had been the designated the Boy Who Lived, how would he have weathered both the unwelcome attention and the pressure of the responsibility? Not as well, I suspect. Harry, even while suffering under the handicap of being raised by the Dursleys, was not cripplingly shy, or plagued by low self-esteem brought on by a psychotic grandmother. I do think Neville would have held up under the burden and eventually grown to deal with it. His response to the burdens in his own life make that a strong possibility. But I don't think it would have been pretty. A Neville Longbottom series would have been a much different set of books.

Neville's journey is different than Harry's, but it's also no less valuable. As Neville moves through Campbell's heroic journey, it's really not surprising that fans have gotten the idea that he is destined for a more important role in the series. And really, in the first three books, either Neville is a one-note incompetent fat kid who exists for the other characters to pity and make fun of, or he's being set up for something else, something greater. There aren't a lot of choices there. And readers with well-developed imaginations who are drawn to fantasy are mostly going to pick the more interesting choice.

Neville fandom is a vast and diverse group. One camp hopes against hope that Neville will turn out to be a major player in the series—that he will become an even bigger character than Harry. Others are just looking for Neville to take on a more heroic role, and hope that his presence in the battles at the ends of *Order of the Phoenix* and *Half-Blood Prince* foreshadow this. Of course some people (and that may be mostly just me) like him the way he is.

MARTHA WELLS is the author of seven fantasy novels, including *Wheel of the Infinite* and the Nebula-nominated *The Death of the Necromancer*. Her most recent novels are a fantasy trilogy beginning with *The Wizard Hunters* and *The Ships of Air*. The last volume, *The Gate of Gods*, will be published by HarperCollins Eos in November 2005. She also has a media tie-in novel, *Stargate Atlantis: Reliquary*, coming out from Fandemonium in February 2006. She has sold short stories to *Realms of Fantasy* and *Black Gate*, and her books have been published in eight languages, including French, Spanish, German, Russian, Italian, Polish and Dutch.

Why Dumbledore Had to Die

THOSE OF US WHO HAVE STUDIED CAMPBELL EVEN MARGINAL-
LY WERE WELL AWARE THAT DUMBLEDORE WAS DOOOOOOOMED.
LAWRENCE WATT-EVANS LAYS OUT THE ROAD MAP FOR THE JOUR-
NEY OF THE MYTHIC MENTOR AND ITS INEVITABLE CONCLUSION,
AND TELLS US WHY THE ROAD LEADS THERE.

> *"After all, to the well-organized mind, death is but
> the next great adventure."*
> —ALBUS DUMBLEDORE, *HARRY POTTER AND THE SORCERER'S STONE*

IN 1976 I WAS AN UNDERGRADUATE at Princeton University and took a course entitled "Myth and Religion," taught by Benjamin C. Ray. One of the highlights of the course was a lecture on James Bond as a heroic archetype—a lecture Professor Ray gave every semester and which was well enough known that it had to be moved to a much larger room than the one the class usually met in, so that students who wanted to hear it but weren't taking the course could sit in.

That lecture was where I first learned the outlines of the universal hero myth, the story Joseph Campbell called "The Hero with a Thousand Faces." For me, as a fantasy writer, that one lecture pretty much justified the cost of the three years I spent at Princeton. Nowadays the idea is familiar to a large percentage of the population, thanks to Bill Moyers' and *Star Wars*' popularization of Joseph Campbell's work, but in 1976 the notion that hero myths follow a standard template was new to me, and I listened to Professor Ray with intense interest.

And after that, anytime I encountered a hero of mythic stature, I just naturally tried to fit him into the mold I had been given by Ben Ray. It usually worked. If a particular hero's story was new to me I could nonetheless predict much of what would happen in it, because that's how "The Story," the universal hero story, always goes.

Was that a problem, that things became predictable? No, the fact that some elements were predictable doesn't mean the stories were boring—it's not *what* happens that matters, but *how* it happens. Lots of genres have standard forms. Every category romance ends with a happy couple, but that scarcely means they're all the same story. You know that in a Hollywood blockbuster the hero will defeat the villain, but you don't know how. A formula is not in itself a story, but merely the frame into which a story fits.

Not every story with a hero in it fits the pattern of the universal hero's, either. There are other ways to construct an adventure. But when you have a character who everyone instantly recognizes as a *hero*, and not merely a protagonist—when that hero's story is immensely popular and resonates with people who ordinarily don't care much about such stories—when the hero has a world and a supporting cast distinctly his own—well, then you're pretty much always going to have that same mythic structure that Professor Ray described on that day in 1976. It's just something in how people in our society think.

When Harry Potter came along, a little over twenty years after I heard that lecture, he was obviously exactly that sort of hero. He fit all the elements perfectly. Here was an outwardly ordinary person leading a boring life in the everyday world who is something more than he appears, and who is drawn from his humdrum existence into a larger world where he becomes the hero he was meant to be, going on to battle a great evil that threatens the world—or at least a part of it.

That description fits Clark Kent stripping off his suit and tie to become Superman. It could also be James Bond being summoned from his cover job in the offices of Universal Export to accept an assignment as Agent 007, or Sir Kay's squire Arthur pulling the sword from the stone to become King of the Britons. It describes Billy Batson saying his magic word to become Captain Marvel, Luke Skywalker leaving Tatooine, Frodo Baggins agreeing to carry the One Ring to Mount Doom—and young Harry Potter leaving his home with the Dursleys on Privet Drive to attend Hogwarts.

The hero is generally an orphan, often with some tragic loss in his background. Superman lost his entire home planet; Bond's background is vague but implied to be unpleasant, and his wife is murdered at the end of *On Her Majesty's Secret Service*; Arthur is an orphaned bastard in a period of civil war; Billy Batson is a crippled, homeless newsboy; Luke Skywalker is told that Darth Vader betrayed and murdered his father and returns home to find the burning corpses of the aunt and uncle who raised him; Frodo Baggins is an orphan whose beloved uncle has gone off to live with the elves; and Harry Potter, of course, loses his parents to Lord Voldemort while just an infant.

113

There are many enemies that oppose these heroes, but one always stands out as the hero's nemesis, his very opposite, whether it's Lex Luthor, Ernst Stavro Blofeld, Mordred, Dr. Sivana, Darth Vader, Sauron or Lord Voldemort.

There are friends who aid the hero, as well—Lois Lane and Jimmy Olsen, Q and Miss Moneypenny, the Knights of the Round Table, the staff of radio station WHIZ, Han Solo and Princess Leia, the Fellowship of the Ring and, for Harry Potter, fellow Gryffindors Ron Weasley and Hermione Granger.

And to fit the classic formula, every true hero must have a powerful and mysterious mentor who will guide him through portions (though only portions) of his heroic journey. Superman has his father, Jor-El; Bond takes his orders from M; Arthur is guided by the wizard Merlin; Captain Marvel's powers were given to him by the wizard Shazam; Luke Skywalker is trained to be a Jedi by Obi-Wan Kenobi; Gandalf sets Frodo upon the road to Mordor; and of course, Professor Albus Dumbledore takes Harry Potter under his wing.

Harry Potter's story fits right in, point for point. It is obvious that in Rowling's seven-volume series we are seeing a new hero in the classic model being added to Western Civilization's already extensive pantheon of heroes.

And thanks to Professor Ray, I know what to expect.

Therefore, when rumors were circulating prior to the publication of *Harry Potter and the Goblet of Fire* to the effect that there would be a death in the story, I assumed it would be Dumbledore.

Instead, of course, it was poor Cedric.

But then there were rumors again, for *Harry Potter and the Order of the Phoenix*, that a character would die, and this time we were assured it was an established and fairly major character.

Again, I thought Dumbledore was doomed. Again, I was wrong.

And in retrospect, it was obvious *why* I was wrong—it was too soon. The climax was still too far away, the young hero still unready for the final confrontation. But by the end of book six, *Harry Potter and the Half-Blood Prince*, Dumbledore's time had run out.

Sooner or later, Dumbledore had to die.

114

Why? You ask *why* I wanted poor lovable Dumbledore to perish? I didn't *want* him to, but sooner or later, he *had* to. Because that's what mentors *do*—once the hero is ready, once he no longer needs them, they die, often voluntarily. They pass away so that the hero can and must stand on his own and defeat his adversary, whoever or whatever it may be, without his teacher's aid and guidance.

That's what makes a hero-in-training into a full-fledged hero, guardian of the world, defender of the weak and all-around good guy—when he takes down the big bad guy all by himself, without a mentor's help.

And he has to *know* he won't get his mentor's help; the hero can't be just trying to hold on until his teacher saves him, he has to know that he's *it*, he's the last line of defense, the man who's got to do the job, no matter what. That's how the story always has to end, with the hero either alone or in command against the foe. He can have sidekicks and companions and friends and assistants and even minions, but he's gotta be the top man, with no mentor to fall back on. It must be *him*, the fated hero, who finally confronts the foe.

That's why the mentor must die—so the hero can't expect his or her help when the chips are down.

The mentor doesn't necessarily *stay* dead, of course, but he or she has to die.

Jor-El stayed on Krypton and perished with his planet—well, in most versions of the story, anyway. (Yes, I know about the Survival Zone story, but in the standard myth Jor-El died when Krypton exploded.)

M...okay, M doesn't die, but M is a title, not an individual, and by the time we meet Bond, Bond is already an experienced agent, not a youth learning the hero trade. And M never leaves London, never comes to help the 00 section in the field.

Merlin doesn't actually *die*, but he's spirited away by Nimue and sealed in a cave for centuries; that's close enough. He's out of the story, in any case.

When Billy Batson first meets the ancient wizard Shazam, Shazam is sitting in a throne in an abandoned subway tunnel with a gigantic stone block dangling from a thread over his head. As soon as Shazam has given Billy his magic powers, the thread snaps and Shazam is crushed. None of this makes any sense at all in real-world terms, but mythologically, it's perfect—the mentor has passed on the burden. When he's done his job it's time to go, so the thread snaps and it's all over instantly. No waiting, no messy delays, just slam down the rock and get it over with. (Mind you, Shazam's ghost hangs around the Rock of Eternity and advises Billy on occasion. As I said, mentors aren't required to *stay* dead. They just need to be out of the picture at the crucial moment.)

Obi-Wan Kenobi dies on the Death Star, allowing Darth Vader to strike him down. He tells Vader that this will make him "more powerful than you can imagine," so he clearly doesn't consider death the end of his mentoring career and, as we see later, it's not—but he's still dead, and Luke can't call on him for help in the final confrontation with Vader and the Emperor and expect a reply.

Gandalf falls battling the Balrog in Khazad-Dum, but he gets better. Of course, Frodo doesn't know about Gandalf's resurrection until *after* the Ring is destroyed—that would spoil his final struggle.

And Dumbledore? Well, right from the first book, as I quoted at the start of this piece, he plainly doesn't see death as a major problem. He's centuries old and ready to rest. He knows, thanks to Hogwarts' many ghosts and portraits, that death isn't necessarily the end of his career. As the hero's mentor, he has his doom written all over him even without these extra details making his death palatable. He has to go so that Harry can save the day single-handedly. Dumbledore *must* die.

It's not that I wished the old man ill; I didn't. Like most of Rowling's readers, I love him. I love all the details we learn about him. I love the fact that he has a pet phoenix named Fawkes and a brother named Aberforth who did inappropriate things with a goat. I admire him for using trading cards as surveillance devices. I'm delighted that he long ago gave up Bertie Bott's Every-Flavor Beans after getting a vomit-flavored one. Little things like these make him one of the most lovable and entertaining mentors in all heroic fiction.

And he certainly does a fine job in the more traditional parts of the role, teaching and defending his pupils, as well. He's generally acknowledged to be the most powerful wizard in Britain, perhaps the world, with the possible exception of Lord Voldemort; it's believed by many people that as long as he's the headmaster at Hogwarts, nothing really dreadful can happen there. He seems to know pretty much everything that occurs anywhere in the wizarding world, and when he deems it advisable he explains virtually anything Harry might want to know. He serves as Harry's guardian, advocate, confessor, confidant and advisor. He is powerful, wise, trustworthy, kindly— almost infallible, really. He's everyone's perfect grandfather figure, a mighty protector and comforter.

And that's why he has to go. Really, with a mentor figure as powerful as Albus Dumbledore in the picture, how can Harry Potter ever prove himself a true hero and single-handedly defeat his nemesis, Lord Voldemort?

If we look back at the other mentor figures, we can see that it's the powerful and lovable ones who always die. M survives, but really, M's just a bureaucrat; the wizards, such as Shazam and Gandalf and Obi-Wan, generally die. They have to, so the hero can win on his own.

The series is about Harry Potter, isn't it? His name is on all the covers; he's the person we follow through each book. He's the hero.

He's not Dumbledore's sidekick; he's the one who's supposed to save the world, all on his own.

So Dumbledore had to die.

And Rowling certainly knew that all along. She gave him that speech in the first book; she established that he's centuries old, that it would certainly be *reasonable* for him to die. Oh, tragic as anything, but still perfectly appropriate. It's a necessary part of Harry's heroic journey.

So at the end of *Half-Blood Prince*, Albus Dumbledore shuffles off this mortal coil, at least to all appearances. He's gone, at least temporarily. He will not be there when Harry faces Voldemort for the last time; the existence of a living Dumbledore, another line of defense against evil, would vitiate Harry's final struggle and triumph. His death adds poignancy and emotional depth. He had to go.

But you know, I liked Dumbledore, so I must admit—I hope he, like all those other mentors, doesn't *stay* dead!

And we've certainly had enough hints that Dumbledore's death may not have been quite what it appeared—this is a wizard who Rowling has associated over and over with the phoenix, a bird that rises from its own ashes. His death came after any number of reminders that magic can fool us, that Polyjuice potion can perfectly duplicate anyone's appearance, that we can't be sure anyone is who he appears to be. *Was* it really Dumbledore that died? If it was, was it a real and permanent death? We don't know yet.

117

There are obvious reasons for Dumbledore to fake his own death— what better way to lure Voldemort out of hiding than to remove the one wizard he fears? There are equally obvious reasons to not let Harry in on the secret. Harry is unwillingly linked to Voldemort, and if the trusting Harry doesn't genuinely believe Dumbledore to have perished, the deception could never fool the suspicious Dark Lord. The whole thing may just be an elaborate charade.

Or perhaps it was indeed Dumbledore who died—but even so, he might have been prepared, with some way to ensure his resurrection in place.

Or he may be genuinely and permanently dead—but that doesn't mean he's gone, any more than Obi-Wan or Shazam are. We already know there's a portrait of him in his office, available to give advice; we already know that wizards who die with unfinished business can survive as ghosts.

We may have seen the last of Albus Dumbledore in person—or we may not have. I don't know what Rowling has up her sleeve for book seven. We can all make educated guesses and try to assemble the hints into a coherent whole, but we won't *know* until book seven arrives.

I can predict a few things with absolute certainty, though, thanks to Professor Ray.

Harry will confront and defeat Voldemort, and he will do so with no wise elder present to assist him—but it will be the lessons he learned from his lost mentor that allow him to triumph, and he will persevere despite all obstacles because to do any less would be to fail his mentor's memory.

That's how the hero's story works. That's how it has always worked.

Whether the mentor returns after the final confrontation, well, that's a variable—but it's a constant that the mentor is not there, *cannot* be there, when the hero confronts his foe and proves himself.

And that's why Dumbledore had to die.

LAWRENCE WATT-EVANS is the author of some three dozen novels and over a hundred short stories, mostly in the fields of fantasy, science fiction and horror. He won the Hugo Award for Short Story in 1988 for "Why I Left Harry's All-Night Hamburgers," served as president of the Horror Writers Association from 1994 to 1996 and treasurer of SFWA from 2003 to 2004 and lives in Maryland. He has one kid in college and one teaching English in China, and shares his home with Chanel, the obligatory writer's cat.

ADAM-TROY CASTRO

From Azkaban to Abu Ghraib

Fear and Fascism in Harry Potter and the Order of the Phoenix

FASCISM IS A HARSH TERM—AND YET, THERE IS NO DOUBT THAT THE TERM FITS MANY OF THE SITUATIONS FOUND IN ALL OF THE HARRY POTTER BOOKS. THIS BECOMES TERRIBLY CLEAR, AS ADAM-TROY CASTRO POINTS OUT, IN THE LATTER THREE. AND CONSCIOUSLY OR UNCONSCIOUSLY, ROWLING HAS SHOWN US OUR OWN WORLD, THROUGH A GLASS, DARKLY, AND IF THE REFLECTION IS A BIT SIMPLER, IT IS NO LESS UGLY.

N YEAR 5, politics enters the world of Harry Potter.

I am not speaking, here, of Harry Potter the fictional universe. Politics was always present there, motivating the power struggles of the wizarding world and complicating the young hero's efforts to survive whatever horrid menace stalked the halls of Hogwarts each semester. It's certainly a major factor in the backstory, though its sheer importance to the narrative as a whole doesn't make itself evident until later volumes.

No, I'm speaking of Harry Potter the brave, principled, much put-upon and increasingly angry boy in the process of becoming a man: Harry Potter who learns that he can be menaced not only by those who want to do him harm, but also by those who find him politically inconvenient. That Harry Potter spends the fifth year of his schooling as a wizard having politics rubbed in his face is appropriate enough given that he's then at a time of life when many bright youngsters are, like him, also developing their first comprehensive understanding that the power struggles of the playground are only amplified by the political give-and-take between adults.

I'm also speaking of Harry Potter the pop-cultural phenomenon of an era when considerations like the extremes our governments are driven to out of fear for their own stability are not just theoretical, but very immediate concerns, which are wreaking a profound effect on the world the young readers and moviegoers thrilling to their hero's adventures will have to face for themselves just a few short years from now. With the fifth novel, that Harry Potter takes on a shape profoundly resonant with the issues we face, not only in the United States (where I write these words and just barely get by), or in Great Britain (where Rowling works and prospers), but through-

out the globe.

This is the year Harry Potter spends trapped between fear and fascism.

Of course, a case can be made that he was already there.

Ethnic politics, often a seed of repression, have always been an issue in the Harry Potter novels. The very issue that Lord Voldemort exploits in his reign of terror, and which motivates the vile Malfoys to support him, is the overwrought sense of entitlement some pureblood wizards use to distinguish themselves from Mudbloods, who have non-magical ancestry, and "Muggles," who possess no magical aptitude at all. The Malfoys (notably described as aristocratic blondes, who wouldn't have been out of place as illustrations of the Third Reich's own hypothetical Master Race) believe themselves guardians of a superior people, sullied by lesser specimens like Mudblood Hermione and the Muggle-sympathizing Weasleys. They consider Voldemort justified in his quest to purify the wizarding race, and eagerly support the first reign of terror that ends with Voldemort's failed attempt on the life of the infant Harry.

Like the real-world equivalent, it's all self-serving claptrap. No-

120

body who ever fought to separate people into superiors and inferiors ever came up with the novel idea of categorizing their own into the ranks of the inferiors. (Somehow, the people who define the categories are always classed on top.) Voldemort's chief ambition is no more profound than the freedom to wreak terror on anybody he dislikes, and the Malfoys want anything that will increase their own wealth, prestige and power. Their bigotry is just an excuse they use to justify their ambitions to themselves. But it's still the nucleus of a movement that ripped the wizarding world asunder in the years immediately prior to Harry's birth and that continues to threaten the world of his adolescence.

There are other manifestations of racial politics. There's the slavery that afflicts the race of house-elves, which goes unquestioned by everybody but Hermione. Even Harry has little problem with this. Oh, yes, he does employ a clever ruse to free Dobby from his cruel master, Lucius Malfoy, in *Harry Potter and the Chamber of Secrets*, but that seems more a stab at Malfoy than any conscientious concern over the civil rights of house-elves. Subsequent developments reveal him as relatively unbothered by the discovery that his beloved school runs as efficiently as it does by keeping a small mob of other house-elves working 24/7 in the kitchen. By the time we get through *Order of the Phoenix* we also know of the wizarding world's despicable treatment of giants and of further discontent brewing among the world's magical creatures, who consider themselves exploited by wizard society. None of this occurs in a vacuum. All of it reflects crimes and resentments going back generations, part of a long and rich history which Harry is just now having explained to him. He's just unfortunate enough to be the focal point of the generation finally forced to deal with it. He is, in short, like all young people, caught up in conflicts that took root long before he was born.

One more background element deserves special mention, before we take up the action of the fifth book. That is Azkaban fortress, a dark and foreboding place where inmates spend years not only physically imprisoned but also afflicted by the proximity of Dementors, whose presence keeps them locked in a constant, crippling state of despair. Few people in the wizarding world question the justice of

121

this cruel and unusual punishment—with the exception of Dumbledore, who quite rightly sees the Dementors as uncertain allies destined to resume their alliance with Voldemort at the very first opportunity. Just about everybody takes it for granted that anybody imprisoned in Azkaban deserves to be there. Nobody bothers to debate it. And yet the first two Azkaban prisoners we meet are the innocent Hagrid (who is sent there briefly for a crime he didn't commit), and the just-as-innocent Sirius Black (who rots there for years, his guilt unquestioned, before escaping as the titular Prisoner of Azkaban). In the end, the very inviolability of the prison serves not justice, but rather the permanence of injustice: another element echoing certain real-life concerns, born in well-known places where the accused spend years locked out of sight without so much as access to defense attorneys. The corruption is inherent in the very system Harry inherits.

Again: this is not his fault.

But it is something with which he has to deal.

Fascism can be defined as what happens when a government treats the people as a threat to its own power. It often occurs when the commonwealth perceives a menace, either internal or external, that operates at least in part by internal subversion, and thus provides an excuse to increase societal repression under the pretext of providing societal security.

It's worth noting that such perceived threats are not always real. They can be wholly imaginary constructs conjured up by mass paranoia, or by political movements that foment mass paranoia in order to cement their own grip on power. Returning to the Third Reich as an example, we find the propaganda Nazi Germany used to portray the Jews of Europe as a race of money-grubbing, politically subversive sub-humans. By painting the activities of the Jews as an immediate threat to the survival of the Fatherland, Hitler and his followers were able to enlist the people of Germany in the creation of a regimented, totalitarian society which the average German accepted as the only legitimate response to ensure the nation's survival. History, in this case and in many others, documents that such a response is often as dangerous to the freedoms enjoyed by any free society as the enemies governments cite as justification.

In the particular case of the Harry Potter novels, the threat of Lord Voldemort is real. But the actual threat that drives *Order of the Phoenix* is fear itself, as manifested by the policies of Minister of Magic Cornelius Fudge. Fudge doesn't believe Voldemort is back. He suspects Harry, and his mentors at Hogwarts, of using rumors to prepare their own power grab. Based only on suspicions of this illusory threat, which on a narrative level functions only as the obstacle hampering our heroes from effectively dealing with the genuine menace, he therefore institutes a series of draconian measures designed to control what he sees as the subversive elements at the wizarding school.

This is also profoundly reminiscent of real-world precedent. Schools and universities have long been seen as the breeding ground of dissent, political activism and open defiance of established orthodoxy. They have therefore long been subject to the tug-of-war between the intellectual freedom that gives young people the tools to question their societies, and the guardians of the status quo who believe students should be taught nothing but loyalty. The debate has been a fixture of every society with an educational system, from the time of Socrates (who was forced to drink hemlock) to the revolt at China's Tiananmen Square (started by students, whose protests were put down by government forces). In extreme cases, the very idea of education becomes an anathema. Witness the Khmer Rouge, who upon taking power in Cambodia began a bloody purge against anybody foolish enough to admit to having an education.

The classic example in the United States is of course campus activism, which reached a peak in the 1960s. The government of the time was not entirely wrong in finding some of these activities dangerous; after all, some organizations that recruited on American campuses saw no problem in advocating, and practicing, violence. Nor were the peaceful activists of the time entirely wrong in distrusting the government, which sometimes employed violence to put down even the trappings of dissent. In one infamous incident out of many, National Guardsmen opened fire on protestors at Kent State, killing four. Even today, long after the fires of that decade have cooled, the battle over the lessons we teach our students still rages, with each side outdoing the other in condemning educators whose lesson plans conflict with their own version of proper political orientation. Look online and you'll find any number of conservative groups with "enemies lists" of professors who teach students to "hate America," and competing liberal groups who take similar exception to professors whose work adheres too closely to a jingoistic, nationalistic orthodoxy. [1]

With all that in mind, it therefore makes perfect sense for the Ministry of Magic to see Hogwarts as a potential den of subversion, run by a politically suspect faculty and attended by a student body that just might be a bunch of fanatic revolutionaries.

Fascism comes in when the pre-emptive steps taken to address this perceived threat do more damage to that body politic than the perceived threat ever could.

124

In the case of *Order of the Phoenix*, those measures make Hogwarts increasingly less a school dedicated to education than a virtual penal institution more interested in keeping its students under strict control at all times.

The first indication of government control of Hogwarts comes on opening day, at which point the Ministry's plant Professor Dolores Umbridge[2] hijacks the banquet to make a turgid speech about "a new era of openness, effectiveness, and accountability, intent on preserving what ought to be preserved, perfecting what needs to be perfected, and pruning wherever we find practices that ought to be prohibited." As with any number of speeches by real-life leaders, the dangerous passages are buried in a sea of indigestible rhetoric. In this case, a promise of "openness" begins the very same sentence that warns about mysterious, and sinister, new prohibitions.

---

[1] I freely admit that I'm bending myself into rhetorical knots trying to be fair here. Like all people with a strong political orientation, I find it much easier to spot the other side being unreasonable than I do acknowledging similar pushiness among my own. That said, given a choice, I'd much rather err on the side of openness, and trust that young people make better decisions when given both sides of the picture, than only allowing them to be taught what they need to know in order to agree with me all the time.

[2] A manifestation of Rowling's great talent for character names, at which she happens to be one of the best since Dickens.

Most Hogwarts students, with the notable exception of Hermione, perceive Umbridge as a boring old blowhard and fail to pay any attention to this early statement of intent. But the density of her rhetoric is the very point: If she spoke her intent in plain language, she'd inflame the opposition at the very start. Her true purpose, here, is not to introduce all of her changes right away, but merely to get a foot in the door.

The thing is, it's perfectly possible for freedom to fail overnight, but it usually takes an invading army. More dangerous fascist movements proceed with caution, instituting their abuses incrementally. One oft-cited metaphor for the way this works is the frog and the pot of water. Toss a frog in a pot of boiling water and it will react to the sudden agony by jumping out if it can. Put the same frog in a pot of room-temperature water and increase the heat by one degree every ten minutes, and the frog won't realize the trouble it's in even as it starts to cook. The principle develops sinister resonance when applied to governments.

125

Professor Umbridge understands this, which is one reason her own adjustments to the curriculum and Hogwarts' power structure function as a series of nested abuses, each one couched in the most beneficial language possible. It's worth noting that if any one of her actions met with effective resistance, the next would not be possible, which is one reason why the earliest are so carefully couched in obfuscatory language.

This is absolutely true of her stewardship of the Defense Against the Dark Arts class, which is no longer the hands-on training of previous years, but a "carefully structured, theory-centered, Ministry-approved course," which has been specifically restructured to discourage students from either obtaining, or using, any practical knowledge. Umbridge couches this as "theoretical knowledge...more than sufficient to get you through your examination, which, after all, is what school is all about." But it's not so much an education as the pretense of one, aimed at pumping out students incapable of challenging the Administration. When the class reacts with predictable anger, Umbridge first places tight controls on who's allowed to speak, then attacks her predecessors as "irresponsible" and (in the case of Lupin) "dangerous half-breeds." Harry's objections result in him being placed under a detention that (he soon finds out) includes torture.

It's Professor McGonagall who warns Harry of the true danger he's in: "Do you really think this is about truth or lies? It's about keeping your head down and your temper under control!" The atmosphere of fear already has less to do with the facts at hand than keeping the obvious questions from being asked.

The outrages continue and grow more, not less, reminiscent of the way things work in analogous real-world situations. There are far too many to relate all of them to their real-world equivalents, but the parallels are so transparent that they hardly need explication to anybody who's ever read a history book or newspaper. Harry's friends are pressured to drop him. The newspaper overflows with stories attacking Harry's credibility: stories that seem to have been written at government behest, by reporters who just take down what they're being told. Those who defend Harry or Dumbledore, or question the motives of the Ministry, are themselves scapegoated: Madam Marchbanks, whose protests appear in one news story, is cited as having "alleged links to subversive goblin groups." Hermione is punished for expressing an opinion that conflicts with the one she's read in her textbook.

Umbridge is given the new office of Hogwarts High Inquisitor, and tasked to question every member of the Hogwarts faculty, prior to a planned purge. She uses this opportunity to direct her full wrath at anybody suspected of sympathizing with Dumbledore, and when she cannot find evidence has no qualms about manufacturing it (at one point filing a negative report about Hagrid that she maliciously concocts on the spot).

There is a real-world name for this kind of agenda. It's called an Enemies List. It condemns not only those who oppose the administration, but also those associated with them. Given full power, an Enemies List can blight the existence of anybody unlucky enough to even know somebody listed there. In Stalin's Soviet Union, and Saddam Hussein's Iraq, people associated with others on such lists could be hauled off to prison on the flimsiest of pretexts; if they were lucky, they merely suffered financial hardships and official harassment. Enemies Lists have also been, unfortunately, in common use in the United States.[3] Senator Joe McCarthy used one to attack people associated with his tally of dangerous communists; President Richard Nixon used one against people who had opposed his administration. With the turmoil of recent years, enemies lists have become ever-more prominent in the mainstream, with many political pundits using them for unrestrained attacks on those whose agendas oppose their own. Accusations of treason are flung again and again against the same short list of names, rendering their very words and ideas beyond the pale, regardless of the points being made.

All of this is consistent with an administration no longer interested in answering questions so much as shutting up the people who ask them. These are the actions of a runaway state, obsessed with its own survival, to the exclusion of all other considerations. When used in schools, in the real world or in Hogwarts, the agenda has less to do with educating students than with raising a class of obedient little functionaries.The dangerous thing, of course, is that there is no bottom line. The more repressive a society becomes, the more repressive it tries to become. There's a steady progression from shutting somebody up to shutting him away, from discouraging certain curricula to outlawing them, from curtailing some rights to taking away all of them. All tyrannies, however long-established, exist in a constant state of experimentation, as they continue to discover what they can get away with next. In Hogwarts under Umbridge, the outrages that here climax in Hagrid under siege are just the beginning of a process that, if allowed to go unopposed, would only have found new depths to plumb. Readers can only shudder at the prospect of just how terrible Hogwarts would have become had Umbridge been allowed to run it unopposed for another five years, or ten, or twenty. Who would be allowed to attend? What would they be taught? And what would the state-approved faculty be free to do to any students who dared to think inconvenient thoughts at an inconvenient time? If Umbridge already engages in torture now, what would she be willing to do in a decade?

127

---

[3] And in Great Britain as well. No major democracy has been entirely free of them.

Terrifying questions.

Were Harry's world, or our world, entirely populated by unquestioning sheep who could be trusted to accept such misuses of power without protest, that would be that.

But tyrannies fall.

And the reason they fall is that people oppose them.

In *Order of the Phoenix*, that opposition takes two forms:

At the urging of Ron and Hermione, Harry recruits a group of trusted students for his own illicit Defense Against the Dark Arts classes. His friends have been brought around to the point of view that they are being shortchanged out of an education they will need to stay alive. It's worth noting that they are doing nothing here but taking charge of their own lives and guiding their own educations. They are risking their futures to learn that which the state, with its current fascistic excesses, would prefer them not to learn.

128

The difference between their situation and that of similar students struggling under repressive regimes in the real world is only that the magical nature of Harry's universe brings the nature of their trespass into startlingly literal relief. Because these illicit lessons *empower* them. These illicit lessons make them *dangerous*. These illicit lessons give them *what they need to survive*. These illicit lessons free them from the empty rote-learning Fudge has mandated to keep them *harmless*. The metaphor here is not accidental. Nor is it accidental that Harry's illicit teachings are, manifestly, not quite as good as those they might have received from a real Defense Against the Dark Arts teacher. Lessons that must be taught in secret, while in hiding, by a teacher not yet fully qualified for the job, are not likely to be as good as lessons taught in the full light of academic freedom. The remarkable thing is that they take place at all, and that they do make a critical difference.

The other major rebellion, a series of spectacular stunts performed by the practical jokers Fred and George, is just as influential. They succeed in making Umbridge look ridiculous and, once caught, reject her authority over them outright, flying off to begin their adult lives, while offering major discounts on their practical-joke equipment to any Hogwarts students who "swear they're going to use our products to get rid of this old bat." The groundswell of public admiration for these pranks makes it increasingly difficult for Umbridge to maintain her position as unquestioned authority figure. After their departure pranks become ubiquitous, and Umbridge is driven ragged trying to maintain her composure in the face of steadily increasing chaos.

And this, too, has a precedent in reality. Nothing hurts an established power figure more than being made to look ridiculous,[4] and the history of resistance movements overflows with incidents where official repression was greeted with guerrilla stunts dedicated to bringing that ridiculousness into sharp relief.

One of the most famous pranks of this kind was the Boston Tea Party, when colonists opposed to the tax policies of the British crown boarded a ship dressed as Indians and poured its entire shipment of tea into the harbor. In the United States, the story is taught anew to each generation of schoolchildren, but (alas) almost always in summary only, with little attention given to explaining exactly why this incident proved such an effective rallying point for the gathering American Revolution, or why it should resonate more than two centuries later. After all, if the point had only been the mere destruction of the tea, there would have been any number of other ways to do it. The ship could have been set afire or damaged in a manner that made it founder. But dressing like Indians—a tactic never intended to shift blame, but rather to echo the stereotype of "noble savage," then the common perception of the natives with whom the Bostonians shared their continent—turned the Tea Party into street theatre, with enormous popular resonance.

Citizens chafing under even the most repressive systems are likely to be alienated, rather than recruited, by genuine terrorism; the same citizens are likely to feel admiration for gestures that deflate the pretensions of stuffed shirts. That kind of rebellion is contagious. That kind of rebellion establishes the authorities as fallible and encourages more of the same. It's the main reason why police in totalitarian countries seem so determined to catch the unknown parties who draw big,

[4] Remember, please, the memorable image Neville Longbottom employs to cope with his own fear of Professor Snape in *Prisoner of Azkaban*.

bushy moustaches on the propaganda posters of El Presidente. The big bushy moustache doesn't hurt anybody, per se. It doesn't inconvenience the government a whit. But it does undermine the government's self-importance, particularly in the eyes of the people, which can be dangerous indeed.

With this in mind, Harry Potter is not the hero of *Order of the Phoenix*, at least insofar as the threat of Dolores Umbridge is concerned. He remains relatively ineffectual against her. There's a reason it feels so deeply satisfying when Fred and George drive her to fury and then blithely fly off, calling her an old bat. They're the ones who demonstrate, by vivid example, that Umbridge cannot remain in power as long as those she seeks to terrorize simply refuse to cooperate with her.

They're the heroes. They're the inspirations.

And it's a good thing they're around to strike the blow.

Because, as a sad Dumbledore notes at the end of the book, "[Harry has] enough responsibility to be going on with."

Politics remain a factor in book six. Fascism is largely out of the picture, at least as far as Hogwarts is concerned. The Ministry that succeeds Fudge's a rather weak one by comparison, deeply committed to surviving the political fallout of the war with Voldemort, but offering the population little but irrelevant safety advisories, publicity-minded arrests of likely suspects, and assurances that they have the situation in hand. They want Harry's endorsement for his propaganda value. There's little evidence that they're equipped to handle Voldemort or anything else. Their activities are far less important, to the actual narrative, than those of their predecessors in book five. But that's the very point. Their focus on image, to the exclusion of all else, renders them irrelevant: also a situation hardly unknown to educated readers. It's worth noting, though, that Dolores Umbridge is still among them, still as hateful as ever—and that she remains a threat as long as there remains a chance of her ever returning to power.

It's a truism that many novels are not only about what they merely seem to be about. A great story is not just an engine to drive the readers from one page to the next. The best are fueled not just by the intangible, often arbitrary rules of make-believe, but by the very same issues that drive the real world inhabited by their authors and readers. Such resonances may not be immediately obvious to those caught up in the stories. But they exist just the same, giving the narratives a weight they might not possess otherwise.

It's worth noting, then, that many of J. K. Rowling's younger readers may not identify Umbridge's behavior as politically repressive so much as single-mindedly mean. They may even leave the book imagining Umbridge's agenda to come from Voldemort, and not the Ministry. There is nothing particularly wrong with this. Everybody absorbs a narrative within the limitations of their own frames of reference, and you don't need to know that L. Frank Baum was commenting on the monetary gold standard to appreciate the comical self-delusion of the denizens of Emerald City in *The Wizard of Oz.*

The fact is, Umbridge *is* mean. Her political agenda completely notwithstanding, she clearly takes great pleasure in her mission to break Harry's spirit, whether that includes attacking his reputation, depriving him of the after-school sport that gives him so much pleasure, or downright torturing him at every opportunity. And she is very much an "ally" of Voldemort, if not in actual fact,[5] then at least in type. Young readers who follow that much, and no more, have absorbed all they really need to thrill to *Order of the Phoenix* as a mere story of a boy caught in a clash between good and evil.

131

But the young readers who see her as nothing more than a mean lady may find additional layers of resonance if they return to the volume later in life. They may even see similarities between Umbridge's behavior and certain figures they find in their daily newspapers.

By then, they might even be voting.

ADAM-TROY CASTRO'S short fiction has been nominated once for the Stoker, twice for the Hugo and five times for the Nebula. His col-

---

[5] The one volume still under composition at this writing may not reveal more to her agenda, but this writer can confidently declare that explaining away her actions as those of a mere Voldemort minion would strike him as tremendously cheap.

lections include *An Alien Darkness*, *Vossoff and Nimmitz* and *Tangled Strings*. His work for BenBella includes essays for the *Alias*, *Hitchhiker's Guide*, *Superman*, *Wonder Woman*, *King Kong* and *Lost* volumes. He is currently working on a book about the TV-reality series *The Amazing Race*, due from BenBella in late 2006, and has also recently completed a novel. All of these will soon be knocked off his shelves by his cats, Maggie the Cat, Uma Furman and Meow Farrow. His beautiful wife, Judi, will just shake her head slowly and try to cope.

Ich Bin Ein Hufflepuff

Strategies for Variable Skill Management in J. K. Rowling's Harry Potter Novels

FROM THE VICES TO THE VIRTUES, THE FOUR HOUSES OF HOG-WARTS EXEMPLIFY BOTH THE BEST AND THE WORST OF THE STU-DENTS WHO ARE "SORTED" INTO THEM. BUT THE SORTING HAT OVERSIMPLIFIES WHAT IS IN EACH AND EVERY STUDENT—IN EACH AND EVERY PERSON, WHEN IT COMES DOWN TO THAT. THERE'S A LITTLE HUFFLEPUFF IN ALL OF US...AND A LITTLE SLYTHERIN, TOO. IT'S HOW WE USE WHAT WE HAVE THAT COUNTS.

THE CARE THAT J. K. ROWLING has taken to validate differ-ent sorts of human genius has been a welcome element of the Harry Potter series since its inception. When the Sort-ing Hat sings its song, it assigns a species of human genius to each of four Houses: aspiration and inventiveness to Sly-therin, valor and courage to Gryffindor, intellectual acuity and learn-ing to Ravenclaw and determination and resolve to Hufflepuff.

At the end of the first Harry Potter book, Professor Dumbledore implicitly describes the accomplishments of our Gryffindor point-of-view characters in terms of these Houses. Ron Weasley wins points to Gryffindor for the "best-played game of chess Hogwarts has seen in many years," a strategic victory that invokes elements of logical analysis (Ravenclaw) and determination (Hufflepuff) as well as the valor of Gryffindor. Hermione wins points "for the use of cool logic in the face of fire," an achievement that clearly invokes Ravenclaw's forte, her intellectual accomplishment enabled by her basic Gryffindor attribute of bravery. Harry's award is for "pure nerve and outstanding courage," the very touchstone of Gryffindor, leaving it up to Neville Longbottom to tip the balance in Gryffindor's favor for a different sort of courage—"the bravery to stand up to his friends," a species of Gryffindor's valor peculiarly suited to the determination of loyal Hufflepuff.

In this way, not only are the attributes of all our beloved point-of-view characters recognized and praised, but the ways in which their Gryffindor natures express and are empowered by other varieties of human genius—all required to achieve success—are validated and admired as worthy of praise.

Hogwarts' Houses reflect different human geniuses or talents: book smarts, people smarts, heart smarts. There's another elemental attribute as important as *what* a person is good at, however, and Rowling's novels give us insight on dealing with *how good* a person is at things, as well.

134

In Shakespeare's play *Twelfth Night*, Malvolio, a comic foil, finds a letter which—among other things—tells him that, "Some are born great, some achieve greatness, and some have greatness thrust upon 'em." He's being set up for a prank of which the Weasley twins could justly be proud; however, in that summary can be found the source of some of the most poignant conflicts in our lives.

Some are born great: talented, beautiful, open-hearted, charismatic. Some achieve greatness through hard work, self-discipline and a passionate desire to perfect their art, their craft or their athletic discipline. Some have greatness thrust upon them by accidents of birth, and must understand the limitations of that social capital in order to have a successful and happy life.

As human animals, one of our life-long concerns is understanding where we fit in, what our roles are and how we stand in relation to others in the multiple hierarchies of our lives. By the time we get to be Dumbledore's age (or the Muggle equivalent thereof, anyway) we've generally made up our minds about where we are and why we're there, and have either reconciled ourselves to our position in life with all of its attendant injustices (like our dear Professor Lupin), or made up our minds to be bitter and angry about it for the rest of our lives (as seems to be the case with Snape). But we all remember our early adulthood, and the pain and anxiety of trying to figure out who we are and where we belong.

In the story of Harry Potter and his friends, Rowling presents us with examples of all combinations of being born great, achieving greatness and having greatness thrust upon us. For the purposes of this discussion, when I say "greatness," I am thinking about a respected and admired place in our human hierarchy. We want people to like us, respect us, admire us and value us. And to a greater or lesser extent we all struggle with the existence of people who have come by privileged positions by an accident of birth or genetics, as Ron Weasley and Draco Malfoy both struggle with Harry Potter's notoriety, each in his own different and instructive way.

Rowling presents positive role models for people across all permutations of that age-old and painful tension between hard work and God-given genius, validating all of those permutations in a life-affirming way that provides encouragement and insight at a critical juncture in younger readers' life journeys. Through the point-of-view characters presented to us in the Harry Potter novels, any one of us has the opportunity to be one of the privileged students at Hogwarts School of Witchcraft and Wizardry, whether or not we happen to be the most famous child in recent history. Let's have a look at how she does it:

Harry Potter himself is the most obvious example of one who has had greatness thrust upon him. When he is introduced to his wizarding heritage he is bombarded on all sides by the admiration and esteem of people who clearly believe that the mere fact of his survival indicates his enjoyment of powers beyond the reach of any ordinary witch or wizard.

Harry has not, however, been "born great" in the sense of being an untutored genius. He's not a particularly good student of—of anything except for Quidditch, in his early years at Hogwarts, and his plight is familiar to any person following in the footsteps of a well-known parent or older sibling, wondering how he is ever going to measure up to such exalted expectations, secretly convinced that he's bound to be a disappointment to one and all.

Though Snape is speaking to a special audience, one can admit to some truth in his characterization of Harry in *Harry Potter and the Half-Blood Prince* as someone who appears to have "no extraordinary talent at all," who "has fought his way out of a number of tight corners by a simple combination of sheer luck and more talented friends," and who is "mediocre to the last degree." Snape's assessment uncovers the fundamental weakness of the Slytherin worldview, however: the confounding of power with strength.

On more than one occasion, but most clearly at the end of *Harry Potter and the Order of the Phoenix*, Dumbledore has affirmed his faith in Harry as an exceptional person. Neither Snape nor Voldemort can find any explanation for Harry's continued survival other than to look for extraordinary powers or assume that he's been lucky. They define Harry in terms of what he can do, while Dumbledore sees him as someone whose intrinsic quality of self is exceptional—exceptionally courageous, exceptional in his ability to affirm life and to love. To the extent that Harry simply is who he is—any question of magical ability aside—Harry Potter has been born great.

136

In the first novel Rowling gives Harry his first self-aware taste of his magical powers when he sets palm to broomstick for the first time. While the text version coyly slides us by with a "Harry's broom jumped into his hand at once, but it was one of the few that did," the filmed version of this scene communicates Harry's surprised pleasure at the success of what seems to be the first magical spell he's gotten right on the first try. Unlike incidents in his past when things happened without Harry's conscious volition, here Harry has not only done something magical but watched himself do it.

Rowling places Harry in the position of someone with genuinely remarkable abilities who can neither understand nor use them without training and guidance—someone who must achieve greatness. In this way she encourages people who may feel that they have no talent: to persevere (in a Hufflepuff sort of a way) bravely (since it takes the courage of a Gryffindor to persist in the face of potential humiliation and failure) in the knowledge that even genius requires a framework and discipline in which to express itself.

Harry Potter was born with superlative talents to which he gains access only as his training progresses. He has had greatness thrust upon him both by public acclaim—first in his role as the Boy Who Lived, then more recently as the chosen one about whom the prophecy was made. Dumbledore intimates on more than one occasion that Voldemort himself has thrust a species of greatness upon Harry, inadvertently transferring power to Harry during the course of his failed attack. And Harry is slowly but surely achieving greatness as his story progresses, and as he adds increasing sureness to talent and innate courage.

His antagonist, Draco Malfoy, has been born great in a different sense; aspires to greatness, building on family pride and privilege; and, in the context of *Half-Blood Prince*, is unfortunate enough to have a sort of greatness thrust upon him at Voldemort's command.

Draco is clearly comfortable in the elitist environment of Slytherin: eager to learn how to manipulate and manage the people around him, conscious of his status as a pure-blood from an old and wealthy wizarding family. He has been fortunate in his birth to the extent that he's had the resources available to him from an early age to learn and practice magical arts, and therefore comes to Hogwarts ahead of the game in comparison to people like Ron—from an old but resource-constrained wizarding family—and Hermione—who has ability and application but no wizarding background at all.

With such a privileged background Draco could clearly become a great wizard (and might still—the story's not over yet). He has been taught to confuse talent and success, however, with strength and power. Gifted with material prosperity and an enriched wizarding background, Draco's been taught to take his privileged status as earned and rightfully his. Growing up watching his Death Eater father kick house-elves around has shaped a young man who can't wait for his opportunity to exercise authority over other people, either as a prefect or a member of the despicable Dolores Umbridge's Inquisitorial Squad.

He is confused, frightened and resentful when he encounters people from less privileged backgrounds whose achievements outshine his own. As unattractive as this may be, isn't it familiar? Any reader whose background is privileged in one way or another is invited to

137

take a lesson from Draco, none of whose material advantages seem to have given him any real edge on anybody—in part because they can confer power, but not strength. The Nimbus 2001 does not make the Seeker, and it is a crucial error to confuse the edge provided by the tool (or the accident of birth which made the tool's ownership possible) with the ability of the one in whose hand chance has placed it.

Material advantage can place an unproved Seeker on a Quidditch team and take an average Quidditch player further and faster than she otherwise might be able to go, but it can't substitute for genius. Life is unfair, and Draco has the choice of working with or against the inequities of fate. So far he has elected to take as much advantage of privilege and position at the expense of talent and ability as possible.

The reader can draw her own conclusions about what that makes Draco Malfoy in the grand scheme of things, but Rowling deploys one of her strongest characters to make her own point. It's not for noth-ing that Dumbledore's strongest feeling appears to be compassionate pity for the boy who has come to kill him. Dumbledore displays a similar, if possibly more contemptuous, pity for Draco's mundane counterpart—Harry's cousin "Dudders" Dursley.

The experience of love and friendship that Harry ought to have had from the Dursleys is received instead from his adoptive family. As grim as Harry's life was between the hour of his parents' death and his first arrival at Hogwarts, there are Weasleys in the story now, and—for all of the contempt so freely expressed by the Malfoys, junior and senior—they're of as old a wizarding family as any.

Ron Weasley has, of course, been far more in the forefront of the novels than the rest of his family, up until *Half-Blood Prince*. In Ron we see how a good-hearted, high-spirited person deals with the fact that he's not as good at things as his buddies are. Hermione is a much better student than either Harry or Ron. Harry's got money, and Ron gets frustrated at being poor. Harry's got the attention and admiration of the masses, and Ron quite naturally would like a little attention and admiration of his own.

In a sense Ron is the positive side of a coin to which Draco Malfoy is the negative side. Where Draco resents Harry's notoriety, Ron thinks it's great—and is quick to defend Harry from envious accusations of grandstanding. Where Draco flaunts his money in front of one and all, Ron doesn't seem to resent the fact that Harry is rich, even while Ron's realistically sensitive to the fact that having a lot of money can be a wonderful thing.

Both Draco and Ron can think, but Draco plots to further his own advantage at the expense of others, while Ron's strategic skills are at the service of the community—consider his chess-playing and sacrifice, so Harry and Hermione might go on, in *Harry Potter and the Sorcerer's Stone*, among other instances. Draco is a bully; Ron, having little power in the world at all, is nevertheless one of Rowling's strongest characters, in more ways than one.

From the beginning Rowling has given Ron his own unique talents and contributions, notably the game of wizard chess in the very first novel, but also Quidditch, among other things. And Ron has always expressed honest admiration for Harry's achievements, largely without the poison of jealousy.

139

Accepting the differences in kind as well as degree between his and Harry's abilities enables Ron to remain Harry's friend, and presents us with one way in which the person who was neither born to greatness nor had greatness thrust upon them may still be genuinely great. In the end, is there anything finer and more to be aspired to than the title of "good friend"? Ron may not be the Sirius Black of the younger generation, all parallels aside, but I don't think there's any question that he is as good a friend to Harry as Sirius was to James Potter.

Ron is not the hero of these books, but his ability to not mind being less well-off, less talented and less famous makes him a paradigmatic good friend—something money, privilege, talent and fame can't buy. We can know and understand Ron's prevailing genius as we get to know him, but Rowling has given Ron the respect and admiration of his peers as well. He is as admired for his learned Quidditch skills, having overcome his insecurities and worked hard, as Harry is honored for the inborn skill that has made him a superlative Seeker. It's interesting to note that their achievements are valued for their contribution to the commonweal—Gryffindor House—and that neither envies the others' success. Weasley is our King by public acclaim, while Malfoy has to settle for buying the more ephemeral respect of his House with material wealth and name-dropping.

There are lots of Weasleys. Taken all in all the family presents a range of different reactions to the combination of actual talent and resource constraint, so let's look at them next. They're nice people, aren't they? Bill's kind of a hippie, but he's happily engaged in forensic accounting of the wizarding kind. Charlie's happy and involved in his work with dragons.

The twins would seem to have no particular genius except that for mischief, and yet the success of their pranks and the quality of their mischief is the clear result of hard work and application, and with hard work and application—identifying their strengths and working toward them, regardless of where they fall on the traditional value scale—they achieve successes, the impact of which resounds far beyond the essentially trivial nature of the niche they have claimed as their own.

140

In an act of courage and daring they risked their savings on a bet to generate a stake, and they were cheated of their winnings by an unfortunate fluke of ill-luck (in *Harry Potter and the Goblet of Fire*). As entrepreneurs they would have continued to seek sources of venture capital aggressively but honorably. In Harry Potter they have found an honest backer, and their successes in *Order of the Phoenix* and previous novels were honestly earned.

By identifying their genius and honoring it, the Weasley twins have discovered their place in life, and—having found that place and making themselves at home in it—they find themselves contributing to the commonweal in more significant ways than they ever imagined. They thought they were just opening a joke shop, but in *Half-Blood Prince* they have discovered that a joke shop can be a much more important weapon for resisting the forces of evil than anything else they could have done.

In this way Rowling validates the strength that comes from finding what you do best and most enjoy, and focusing on it. The Weasley twins are not necessarily powerful wizards. They have simply concentrated on making the best of what powers they have, and leveraged their skills to become a powerful force for good. They have achieved, and are in the process of achieving further, greatness.

So what happened with Percy?

Percy has ambition. Ambition is good, but his ambitions appear to exceed his actual abilities, and have made him vulnerable to exploitation. Rowling shows us what kind of compromises Percy's made to reach for privilege that exceeds his ability to earn it. His desire for the material benefits of rank—money, influence, a position of power—appears to have destroyed his objectivity.

He has estranged himself from his family, which is a very strong message in Rowling's world—where Harry is safe from the worst that Voldemort can throw at him when he's with Aunt Petunia, because Aunt Petunia is his mother's sister. There are ways in which Percy shows the worst effects of Voldemort's poison: Whether or not his behavior has anything to do with evil wizards, there is an uncomfortable harmony between what he has to say to his family and the curses Sirius Black's mother calls down upon the heads of the Mudbloods.

Percy may yet pull himself out of the quagmire (there's part of me that can't help hoping he's working on a long-term, Dumbledore-derived stratagem), but until then he's Rowling's reminder that profoundly misguided people can come out of the most fundamentally decent families, wizard or no, and are capable of causing quite as much grief as they could have had they talent in proportion to their ambition.

While magic apparently runs in families like the Weasleys, there's no guarantee that magic parents will pass on their single most distinguishing characteristic and have magic offspring. Some children of wizarding parents are born Squibs, having no magic power whatever of their own, and deal with that either more (Mrs. Figg) or less (Filch) successfully. To balance it out, sometimes outstanding magical ability is discovered in a family with no prior history of magic, as was apparently the case with both Harry's mother and Hermione Granger.

Hermione is a fish out of water in a classic sense, like a student who's been skipped a grade or placed in any enriched learning environment. Her family background is materially privileged to an extent: her parents are dentists. This means a lot of hard work on their part, however, and a sensible notion of economic constraint that is closer to Ron's family than Draco's, for instance. There is no wizarding in her background, and in that she is more like Muggle-raised Harry than anyone else in the book, except of course for Voldemort himself.

What I recognize most about Hermione, though, is that she is ambitious and intellectually voracious while wanting to be liked and fit in, and is confused and frustrated by the fact that she is not and does not. Hermione is the most Ravenclaw of the Gryffindors we know, and bright students in today's academic environment need all of the Gryffindor they can get to face the challenges of their lives.

Hermione is more vulnerable to Slytherin elitism than anyone else in the series. She has the intellectual capacity; she has the determination and the ambition to succeed. She could easily despise Harry for his apparent lack of ambition, Ron for being lazy, everybody in Gryffindor for being less dedicated students. Feelings of easily demonstrated superiority in nearly every aspect of wizard academics could be easily substituted for her feelings of anxiety and confusion over wishing to be liked and to fit in, and would be considerably less painful.

Under these circumstances it is Hermione's act of courage to decline to scorn, and to continue to value, the friendship of people who can't match her on an intellectual level. Hermione's intellectual achievement is to no mean extent in her recognition of the fact that the intellect is only part of a range of human geniuses.

At first reading, I found Hermione's "friendship and bravery" speech at the end of *Sorcerer's Stone* to be an embarrassing bit of authorial cheerleading. In light of Rowling's subsequent books, however, I think it's a deliberate statement of an enduring human truth about different sorts of genius and what it takes to maximize them all.

Because Hermione, as well as Ron, does something else that demonstrates her strength: She fits herself to the service of others who have the power that she lacks, but who cannot access that power without her assistance. Hermione uses her abilities to maximize her friends' strengths toward a common goal. For all of Hermione's genuine wizarding talent, her true genius may well be in the Muggle art of teamwork.

Every reader of Harry Potter will be able to recognize familiar talent-versus-training conflicts in one or more of the characters that Rowling has taught us to know and love. We all know how it feels to have a natural knack, how it feels to be unable to get the knack no matter how hard we try, and how frustrating and unfair it can be to be compared to other people who are accidentally or innately just plain better (more knackful?) at things than we are. We have all faced the challenge of how to respond to being better and not as good. Rowling's characters demonstrate how to respond to all of these life-challenges in positive and honorable ways.

Rowling shows us how a Hermione manages her pride and her humility in order to remain a friend, a partner and a life-affirming person. She shows us how Harry can manage his frustration at his lack of background and training without developing the corrosive "I'll show them" desire to make others feel inferior. She shows us mistaking material privilege for moral superiority has bred up a weak and flawed character in Draco Malfoy, and how the most powerful wizarding traits are common to Muggles and magical folk alike—integrity, honor, loyalty, friendship and the transcendent power of love.

143

At the end of it all, J. K. Rowling has given us all ways in which to take whichever species of human genius we've got, in whatever degree we've got it, and fit ourselves with it into a just and ordered society focused on the common good. It's a lesson that can benefit people across the entire spectrum of talent, genius and position in life.

I was born of the Muggle equivalent of a respectable middle-class wizarding family. Compared to some my upbringing was enriched; compared to others, it was impoverished. Compared to some I was an academic success across all spectra except athletics; compared to others I had talent, but not genius, and could only watch the workings of the minds of truly brilliant scholars with appreciation and awe. Compared to some I have had great success in my life, while compared to others I am a small fry indeed.

When I first read Harry Potter it seemed to me that Slytherin was the place to be, and Gryffindor was a sorry second; of Hufflepuff and Ravenclaw I knew nothing, and had an equivalent opinion. J. K. Rowling, by demonstrating the attributes of each House within the characters she has placed in Gryffindor, has taught me differently: not only in terms of the House attributes themselves, but in terms of where I fit in the human spectrum of talent, genius and aptitude.

Some are born great, some achieve greatness and some have greatness thrust upon 'em—and it's never too late for the latter two of those three states. With the examples Rowling has presented of how a person with modest talents, some charisma and a strong sense of community can find her place among people smarter or better or harder-working (or even richer) than she is, I can claim my proper place, and be well pleased with it. *Ich bin ein Hufflepuff*, and I know how to bloom where I've been planted. It's good to find the place where I belong, and understand how my being there is what makes it possible for Harry and Hermione and Ron to exercise their own human and wizarding geniuses for the common good of us all.

144

SUSAN R. MATTHEWS was born in a barracks in Fort Benning in the middle of a windstorm whose chaos has characterized her life ever since, most of which has occurred while she was paying attention to something else. She has been most recently seen in science fiction and murder mystery anthologies; her next Koscuisko novel, *Warring States* (whose protagonist would almost certainly have been sorted into Slytherin the moment he set foot to flagstone at Hogwarts), is due out from independent publisher Meisha Merlin in January 2006.

Susan lives in Seattle, Washington, with her partner Maggie and two Pomeranian doggies. She has yet to quit her day job at The Boeing Company, where she enjoys a regular paycheck, health benefits and other Muggle perks, and is convinced that the reason You-Know-Who is determined that nobody kill Harry Potter but him is that Harry Potter *is* the final Horcrux.

Harry Potter as Schooldays Novel

FOR THOSE WHO ARE, IN THIS DAY AND AGE, UNFAMILIAR WITH THE TRADITION OF THE BRITISH SCHOOLDAYS NOVEL, JAMES GUNN FILLS US IN ON JUST WHAT THE GENRE IS AND WAS, AND HOW ROWLING HAS ADAPTED IT FOR AN ODD SORT OF TWENTY-FIRST CENTURY.

N O ONE KNOWS what makes a bestseller, much less what makes a publishing phenomenon like the Harry Potter novels. Some experts claim to know: According to legend, Hervey Allen's agent told him that it was time for a long historical novel, and Allen then wrote *Anthony Adverse* (1933). But agents give advice to authors every day, and few bestsellers emerge.

Explanations for the success of the Harry Potter series range from the trail-blazing influence of such fantasy classics as J. R. R. Tolkien's Lord of the Rings trilogy and Ursula K. LeGuin's Earthsea trilogy, to its positioning as a young adult fantasy, bringing the delights of the imagination to the school-age reader. But while J. K. Rowling's invention, story-telling and sympathetic characters have received a good deal of critical praise, not enough attention has been paid to the series' use of basic popular appeals.

The late John Ciardi once described fiction as "character under stress"; another writer called it "interesting people in difficulties." These definitions may be too succinct to be definitive, but the Harry Potter series satisfies both: certainly Harry faces the desperate challenge of finding his parents' killer and preventing evil from taking over the world, as well as surviving the everyday problems of the Hogwarts School of Witchcraft and Wizardry.

The situation and portrayal of Harry as an ordinary child with an extraordinary talent make him interesting. He elicits our sympathy at every turn. He plays a Cinderella-like role as the abused child of mean-spirited foster parents who favor other, less-worthy children, and also fits another fantasy role, that of the changeling. Millions of children have nursed the notion that they cannot be the offspring of such unremarkable parents; in the Harry Potter books, the metaphor is often literal truth.

Reading about children in situations like these makes us care. There is special resonance, however, for the child who feels misunderstood, discriminated against and made of finer stuff than his or her family. Early on, Harry is offered the glass slipper of appointment to Hogwarts. He actually is a changeling, so different from his loutish cousin and his abusive aunt and uncle that fairy godmother Hagrid comes to liberate him and take him to the ball. Well, not to the ball, of course, but the school. And that is where his real challenge begins. He is the "chosen one," a role that is forced upon him, and its burden is one he must bear. Being chosen in this fashion is not uncommon in fantasy fiction, but seldom with a child so young and inexperienced, one so unprepared by his upbringing to accept his unique powers and position, develop them and use them wisely.

His challenge is not just to find his parents' murderer before he himself is killed, but to prove himself and discover his talents in a school filled with strangers—both instructors and classmates—some of whom will turn out to be mentors and friends and some of whom will become rivals and enemies. Sometimes the challenge lies in recognizing the difference.

No one seems to have observed that Harry Potter is merely a variation on the English schooldays novel, which got its start in 1857 with Thomas Hughes' *Tom Brown's Schooldays* and Dean Frederic W. Farrar's lesser-known 1858 novel *Eric*. Although they were not the first of their kind, these two novels established the conventions for what became an entire genre.

146

Tom Brown's Schooldays was a critical and popular success, with fifty editions printed by the time of Hughes' death in 1896. It has seldom been out of print since. It also has been filmed several times. The novel, published anonymously ("by an Old Boy"), was written for the author's eight-year-old son before the boy started at Rugby School. Hughes himself had attended Rugby, under Headmaster Thomas Arnold,[1] for nine years, becoming captain of both the cricket and the rugby football teams. Arnold had helped transform the so-called public schools of England, abolishing the flogging and brutality of the previous generation in favor of a system that concentrated on a classical education and its product, the "Christian gentleman." In the process, he elevated the position of headmaster to one of prestige and influence.

Hughes, on the other hand, was far more interested in sports as the way to produce "muscular Christians" (a term attributed to Hughes' close friend, the writer Charles Kingsley[2]). Tom Brown's father, like the actual author, put morality first, and he thought morality emerged from team sports. "If he'll only turn out a brave, helpful, truth-telling Englishman, and a gentleman, and a Christian," the elder Brown reflected, "that's all I want."

Much of Tom Brown's experience at Rugby dealt with his moral development: he passed through the stages of "fagging" (serving and running errands for the older boys), was bullied until he stood up for himself, participated in sports, got into fights and cheated...until he promised a dying friend he would reform and became a model English gentleman. According to Isabel Quigly, who critiqued schooldays fiction in *The Heirs of Tom Brown*, the novel established public schools as institutions for educating the middle-class bureaucrats the British Empire needed. By condemning young boys to spend their childhoods among strangers, the system better prepared them

[1] Matthew Arnold, one of Thomas Arnold's eleven children (two died in infancy), attended Rugby with Thomas Hughes. He became a noted poet ("Dover Beach") and scholar, defending the classical education against such innovators as Thomas Huxley, who wanted English universities to include science in their curriculums. Matthew Arnold also wrote "Rugby Chapel" as a defense of his father's image.

[2] Kingsley was the author of *Westward Ho!* and *Water Babies*. Kingsley and Hughes were prominent Christian Socialists who emphasized the social content of the Christian message. Hughes used his own money to set up a utopian community in Tennessee and spent four years there between 1878 and 1882.

to serve the Empire for decades in foreign climes. But at what cost! One can imagine a child of eight or nine being thrust from his or her family and sent off to dormitory exile for years—what must these children have felt? What must their families have felt? Sometimes the trauma marred them for life. Those for whom the process succeeded went abroad in service to the Empire, married late (if at all) and sent their children back to England at an early age to undergo the same experience.

Eric's author, Farrar, was one of these children. Born in Bombay, India, Farrar was sent back to England, along with his older brother, at the age of three. There the two attended King Williams College on the Isle of Man as boarders. Farrar then went on to Trinity College, Cambridge, where he was awarded a scholarship, and received his BA at the age of twenty-one from King's College, London. Unlike Hughes, he was a scholar, earned a Masters at Marlsborough, was ordained a deacon at the age of twenty-three and became a priest at twenty-six. He was elected a fellow at Trinity, and became a housemaster at Harrow, Canon at Westminster and later Chaplain of the House of Commons.

148

When Farrar wrote *Eric* in 1858, he was twenty-seven. Eric, like Farrar, was sent to England from India and attended Roslyn School on the Isle of Man. Like Tom Brown, Eric had trouble getting along, is often tempted by "cribbing" and playing games, which distracted him from his studying, and is redeemed by a dying boy whose life he saves, turning to scholarship and good deeds. But he is then disgraced when he is falsely accused of cheating, signs on to a sailing ship, gets ill and dies. Where Hughes emphasized the value of games in developing the English gentleman, Farrar considered them a temptation. *Eric* praised scholarship and, according to scholar P. W. Musgrave in his 1985 study *From Brown to Bunter: The Life and Death of the School Story*, dealt with the way "in which Christianity should govern morality amongst the middle class."

Succeeding novelists often incorporated school chapters, including Mrs. G. Linnaeus Banks' *The Manchester Man*. The famous Anthony Trollope wrote *Dr. Wortle's School*, and the less well-known Mrs. Henry Wood, the three-volume *Orville College*. Other writers added to the genre: W. H. G. Kingston, Talbot Baines Reed, H. C. Adams, T. S. Millington, A. R. Hope and Ethel C. Kenyon, among others. Baines in particular established genre expectations with schooldays stories he wrote for the *Boy's Own Paper*. More famous are a collection of school stories by Rudyard Kipling, called *Stalkey and Co.*,[3] and Alec Waugh's *The Loom of Youth*, about his four years as a boy at Sherbourne. P. G. Wodehouse wrote *Mike* and then *Mike and Psmith* before moving on to those works for which he became famous. In the latter he satirized the conventions of the schooldays story by having Psmith ask Mike, "Are you the Bully, the Pride of the School, or the Boy who takes to drink and is led astray in Chapter Sixteen?"

The popularity of the schooldays novel, like that of the Harry Potter series, may result from its tapping into the universal experience of being forced from the security of the home into the terrifying outer world, with its unprecedented demands for discipline and new power structures. The kindergarten youngster clinging to his or her mother before being torn away and abandoned to the tyranny of the schoolroom is a familiar image. In the British schooldays novel, the institution of the boarding school made the separation even more traumatic. So many middle-class Englishmen had gone through the ordeal that the act of reading or writing schooldays stories was both cathartic and nostalgic, allowing former schoolboys to both reassure their anxieties and relive their triumphs.

By 1929, the genre had begun to suffer from the diminishing of shared goals and publishing criteria to the point where one reviewer commented in the *Times Literary Supplement*, "The once fairly plentiful output of stories of school life has been shrinking in recent years and this year the number is small enough to raise a question whether the shrinkage is a symptom of some real change in the taste of modern boy readers." By 1940, one year into England's involvement in World War II, the genre was already considered dead. The British Empire was fading away, and the British boarding school itself, where it persisted, wasn't the same ordeal it had previously been.

Although schooldays fiction was most common in England be-

---

[3] John Rowe Townsend, in *Written for Children*, calls *Stalkey and Co.* "almost anti-school story, not a typical one." Indeed, he believes, "its cynicism damaged the genre," and contributed to its decline.

cause of its public-school traditions, novels that dealt with schooling were also prevalent in the U.S. A favorite example was the Frank Merriwell novels, serialized around the turn of the century in Street & Smith's *Tip-Top Weekly*, a magazine for boys created after the demise of the dime novels. The Frank Merriwell novels, by Burt L. Standish, were reprinted as cheap paperbacks, and one of the high points of my youth was when my father took my brother and me to an upstairs closet and pointed toward a high shelf that held fifty or more of the Merriwell books. I read my way through them more than once. The last I remember of them was a disintegrating mound of pulp paper in a cloth-covered chest.

The early novels described Frank's life at Farwell Academy. Much like Tom Brown, he excelled in sports—although his were baseball and football—but he was seldom tempted, unlike Tom, to stray from the paths of rectitude. He had schoolboy enemies and always had to overcome great odds, but his skills[4] and good character always won out. He was even a bit *too* good; I must admit a fondness for his "fun-loving brother," Dick,[5] who later followed in his brother's footsteps. So popular was Frank, however, that when he graduated from Farwell and chose to continue his education at Yale, applications to Yale increased tenfold.

150

Another series of American schooldays stories, the *Lawrenceville Stories*, which Owen Johnson wrote for *The Saturday Evening Post*, featured Lawrenceville Academy. These stories were later collected into seven volumes (including *Stover at Yale*) and, like *Tom Brown's Schooldays*, filmed frequently.

All of these are only the tip of the iceberg.[6] They describe a type of fiction most popular during a specific period of English history, fiction that was a direct response to the social and political situation in which its readers and writers lived. The universally difficult experience of enrolling in a new school continues to give the schooldays

---

[4] He had a favorite pitch—a "double shoot" that curved in and then out.

[5] Dick tried to acquire his brother's "double shoot" but was able only to throw a ball that dipped up and then down!

[6] C. S. Lewis' Narnia novels, for instance, include one—*The Silver Chair*—in which Eustace and a schoolmate escape boarding school when summoned by Aslan, and *Prince Caspian* begins on an abandoned train platform. Both books detail escapes into fantasy from the dreadful realities of school.

books resonance when they are read today, but the genre grew out of the practices of a particular time and place, and were of special interest to those who had been sent to boarding schools themselves as young children—sometimes as young as seven or eight.

Author Brian W. Aldiss described his experience In *Hell's Cartographers*: "What happened to me at eight was a terrible thing. I have so far painted a cheerful picture. At the age of eight, I was sent away to boarding school, and at boarding school and public school I remained until I was seventeen and old enough to go into the army—whereupon I was promptly whisked abroad to the Far East for four years. So my severance from home and parents began early in life, far too early."

Aldiss was not alone. Author Osbert Sitwell wrote: "Suddenly, just when they have reached an age when their intelligence and sensitiveness...can respond to the stimuli of their surroundings, they are whisked off to places of dreary internment, called private—though now more widely known as prep—schools, where the most extraordinary tribal values and standards prevail...until such time as their characters have been formed into the same dense, hard and unpleasant mould as that of those who teach them." Diarist James Lees-Milne: "My parents arranged for me to go to school. It was, they decided, high time, for I was already well over eight years old. Convention demanded that little boys should be wrenched from home at this age and dumped among a hundred others in a grim institution as unlike home as could be devised." Poet and journalist Edward Lucie-Smith: "By this time I was eight, and it was time to send me to boarding school. It was not an event I looked forward to with much confidence.... I was convinced that school would be a place of imprisonment and terror. By and large, my somber expectations were fulfilled."

Not everyone felt that way. Those for whom the process worked formed lifelong attachments. According to novelist Robin Maugham, "Eton was a way of life....Etonians never left Eton; they merely changed into being Old Etonians." Satirist, Catholic and detective novelist Ronald Knox said when he left Eton that he "felt as if he were going into exile," and his biographer, Evelyn Waugh, discussing the illness Knox had suffered just before leaving school, re-marked that "if he had died then, it would have been at the apogee of his worldly glory."

Isabel Quigly, in *The Heirs of Tom Brown*, speculated that English life at that time demanded this kind of sacrifice from the children of the privileged class: "The strengths and limitations which ten years of such schooling produced were exactly those needed by imperial functionaries; and not only by them but by the many British who, in the public-schools' century, went about the world as civil engineers, as businessmen, as openers-up of new places, administrators of old ones. A boy with ten years' training (five at preparatory, five at pub-lic school) could face things that would daunt the untrained: loneli-ness, isolation, tough living conditions, the lack of home comforts, above all removal from all that was familiar: his own home, country, culture, family and friends. If at eight such removal was thrust upon him, at eighteen he would consider it normal." Perhaps the same re-marks could be applied to Harry Potter, who it seems is being pre-pared for a final sacrifice.

152

If the schooldays genre faded away in 1940, as most scholars be-lieve, it may have been due to not only the shock and cultural dis-ruption of world war and the changing times, but also the collapse of the British Empire. While the genre was in style, it offered writers an opportunity to write about (and possibly deal with) formative ex-periences of their youth. As a fictional pattern, they provided an un-paralleled structure on which to hang a story.

As John Rowe Townsend said in his chapter on "School Stories" in *Written for Children*, "School is a self-contained world in which boys—or girls—are full citizens. At home a boy is only a subordi-nate member of his family....But at school the boy is standing on his own feet: he must hold his own among his contemporaries; he is responsible for himself. The school story thus gets over one of the first problems of any realistic literature for children: how to make the characters full participants in the life of their community."

Townsend goes on: "Then school life is full of moral issues: the familiar problems like bullying, cribbing, and sneaking, and the less familiar but more interesting ones that arrive out of conflicting loyalties to the group, to one's friends, and to oneself.... The clash between authority and the individual is the stuff of a great deal of drama, and for young people the school is an ideal setting in which to show it."

What does all this have to do with Harry Potter? The Harry Potter novels are fantasy, but their appeal is based on their grounding in real-life experience, including being sent away from home (even if, in Harry's case, it is a sorry home and he is eleven, not eight) and plunged into an overwhelming experience at a new school filled with potentially antagonistic strangers. To be sure, Hogwarts is not your typical Rugby or Roslyn. It is coeducational, for one, and its subject matter is scarcely traditional. Harry, in fact, comes to love it—at the end of the first film (*Harry Potter and the Sorcerer's Stone*), on the train platform ready to return to his family, he says, "I'm not going home." Hogwarts has become his home. Nevertheless, the emphasis of the Harry Potter novels on games (Quidditch anyone?), competition between Houses (students can win or lose points—for their House) and tradition (the medieval architecture and the menacing portraits), as well as its wise headmaster, ambiguous housemasters and teachers, and preoccupation with the basic business of making friends, dealing with enemies and simply figuring out what is going on and how to survive it, place the story firmly within the realm of the schooldays story.

Rowling draws upon the conventions of an old genre in *Harry Potter*; it appeals to the experiences of every child who is or ever has been thrust into the unknown and untested world of school, and every adult who remembers the experience. It is revealing that adults long out of school still have nightmares about the class they have never attended, the test for which they have never studied, the school play for which they have forgotten the lines, the game they lost or the bully who assaulted them and what they should have said or done....

England's private school boarders were being prepared for service to the Empire; what are students at Hogwarts being prepared for? Perhaps for the empire of the enlightened, as opposed to the boring mundanity of Muggles? Or their role in preventing the forces of darkness from establishing its own empire? Are the students, sent off to school at an early age, being hardened for a place on the front lines? Are they being not only taught but tested?

Hogwarts prepares its pupils for a different kind of challenge. Some will interact with the Muggle population, some (like Percy Weasley) will fill dreary desk jobs at the Ministry of Magic, and some, like their Victorian-era real-world predecessors, will travel the world, dealing with alien populations and dangerous places—think of Bill Weasley, working as a curse-breaker in Egypt for the goblin-owned bank Gringotts, or Charlie Weasley, working with dragons in Romania. And some will, as Harry plans to, become Aurors, able to identify and thwart Dark Wizards. They in particular are the front line in a war being waged against those who would use the Dark Arts to hurt others and gain power.

In many other ways the Harry Potter novels echo the school-days genre. Draco Malfoy tells Harry in *Sorcerer's Stone*, in a tone not meant to be trusted, "You don't want to go making friends with the wrong sort." Hermione says at the book's end, "There are more important things—friendship and bravery," a sentiment echoed by Headmaster Dumbledore, "Love and courage."[7] Like Thomas Arnold, Dumbledore stands aside and lets Hogwarts students deal with arrant unfairness, like Snape's partiality, on their own—they will have to deal with worse in the world that comes after school. Finally, Harry is more of a hero, specifically a sports hero, than a scholar. Hermione is a better student, and Ron, a better chess player. It is Harry who gets the others into difficulties by disobeying the rules— although always for the best reasons. Tom Brown would not have done it differently.

I would like to venture the heretical notion that the Harry Potter novels would be just as engrossing without the magic—not, perhaps, the publishing and audience phenomenon they became, but just as involving a narrative. The magic is the icing on the cake, or the embroidery on the pillowcase—it may be what sells the series, and even what elevates the stories into the extraordinary, but without the un-

---

[7] Or at least that's how it sounds at the end of the first movie. He may, in his British accent, be saying "nerve and courage," as in the book.

derlying structure of the schooldays genre supporting it, the series would lose its fundamental appeal.

Maybe the schooldays genre is not dead after all.

JAMES GUNN is an emeritus professor of English at the University of Kansas, and director of its Center for the Study of Science Fiction. He is the author of a dozen novels, half a dozen collections of stories and a dozen books about science fiction, as well as the editor of nearly a dozen anthologies.

155

Harry Potter and the Post-Traumatic Stress Disorder Counselor

POOR HARRY! J. K. ROWLING TRULY SUBSCRIBES TO THE EDICT THAT A GOOD BOOK IS ONE IN WHICH YOU CREATE CHARACTERS THAT THE READERS LOVE AND IDENTIFY WITH—THEN DROP A MOUNTAIN ON THEM. OR, IN THE CASE OF POOR HARRY, AN ENTIRE MOUNTAIN RANGE.

And then, without warning, Harry's scar exploded with pain. It was agony such as he had never felt in all his life....
—*HARRY POTTER AND THE GOBLET OF FIRE*

This was the worst he had ever felt.
—*HARRY POTTER AND THE CHAMBER OF SECRETS*

I LOVE THE HARRY POTTER BOOKS. I want to establish that, first and foremost. I have all of them, and I began my reading of them with a certain amount of skepticism (something that popular can't be that good) and read each new one with the same eager anticipation as a member of the audience for whom it is intended. I even own the Hats—Sorting, Madam Hooch's and Professor McGonagall's.

However, I am also an adult writer of fantasy...and as such, I can no longer simply read something without the little critic in the back of my head going, "You must be joking." Most of the folks in my household are the same way...which is why one evening in a fit of lunacy, we invented the "Harry Potter Drinking Game."

Now you probably know what a drinking game is—an exercise designed to lure you into consuming more alcohol than is good for you, on the basis of the occurrence of an event that seems as if it will occur with less frequency than it actually does.

So, here it is—and may Joanne Rowling forgive me for it.

Whenever Harry responds to a long and complicated question with a monosyllabic "Yeah," take a drink.

On the surface of it, this really does appear to be a major flaw. But I've since spent some time eavesdropping on teenage boys.

They actually do this. That is, when they respond at all. Very often the long and complicated question is greeted with silence, rolling eyes, a sigh or all three.

So while this is still justifiably part of the drinking game, score one for Rowling for getting it right.

Whenever Harry's anatomy spontaneously rearranges itself, such as his heart making scenic migrations to various parts of his body like his feet and his throat, take a drink.

All right. We all do this. We have phrases we overuse. Mine used to be, "He looked like someone had hit him in the back of the head with a board." But when they occur often enough to become part of a drinking game—

Critic One, Rowling One.

On a side note, we include in this part of the game the signature phrase, "He felt a small jerk behind his navel." We would like to know (this is the household, not the royal "we") just who this small jerk is and what he is doing behind Harry's navel.

This brings me to the final part of the game.

Whenever Harry experiences "the worst pain ever felt in his life," take a drink.

Now, this made me stop and think.

We as writers are basically in the business of inflicting trauma on our characters, and Harry comes in for far more than his share when compared to, say, the average boarding-school pupil. Hence the title of this essay: after the events of only the first book, a normal kid would be seeing a shrink, and we're not done yet. We begin the first book with Harry living in a profoundly abusive situation. He spends most of the time when he's not acting as an indentured servant, living in a closet full of spiders under the stairs. The child in me is shivering with sympathetic *schadenfreude*. The adult and writer in me is going, *Where the heck is Child Welfare?* The Dursleys are patently not fit to raise a poodle; didn't *anyone* in the wizarding community check these people out before delivering a helpless kid into their hands? And surely, if they can deliver letters and even parcels by owl, they could and should have been checking up on him.

For that matter, what about the Muggle community? Teachers are supposed to be trained to watch kids for signs of abuse. You would think that a competent teacher would have seen the signs of abuse in Harry before the boy got out of second grade.

In the later books, we get a flimsy explanation about the nature of the magic protecting him, and for the critical adult, it just feels like an afterthought. The adult is not convinced.

But there is a long tradition in English literature of putting children in awful situations for the sake of the story. Even in children's books. Roald Dahl was the past master at this sort of plot—*James and the Giant Peach*, for instance—and before the Harry Potter (and now Lemony Snicket) books came out, one could make the case that he had pretty much cornered the modern market on the abuse of young children for the sake of a story.

The tradition goes back a lot further, of course. The Victorians loved this sort of plot, and the use of it ranges from the best (*Oliver Twist*, for instance) to maudlin little tracts in which an unrealistically good child suffers unspeakable abuse and remains good, often dying in the end and going to heaven.

However, Roald Dahl's books are fantasy and have an obviously fantastic setting, and Dickens is in the past, where unspeakable abuse to children wasn't given the attention it is now, but in this day and age, abuse like that should not have escaped the eye of teachers and fellow students. And in fact, in the case of dumping infant Harry with these patently awful people, an adult is often left wondering: *What were they thinking?* Rowling One, Critic Two, I think, so far as an adult reader having trouble suspending disbelief in the Dreadful Dursleys goes.

However, this is not the sort of thing that would make young Harry a candidate for a PTSD counselor. Not yet, anyway.

Now, having one of your favorite teachers turn out to be a literally two-faced monster, controlled by the creature that murdered your parents—

That would make *anyone* eligible for PTSD counseling.

But by this time, of course, we are well into the fantasy portion of the plot, and it is a lot easier for the adult reader to simply fall into the story. Rowling Two, Nitpicky Critic Two.

By book two, Harry is well into the realms of stresses that would make anyone crack. He's sent back to the Dursleys and on return for his second year finds himself the focus of a whispering campaign by the denizens of House Slytherin, which—even without the trauma— is grounds for paranoia and a persecution complex besides.

Once again, Fussy Critic raises her ugly head. The adult disconnect here is this: Slytherin harbors more malcontents than a Russian bar when the vodka has run out, and has been the breeding ground for Lord Voldemort and all his Death Eaters, and still Hogwarts allows it to remain.

Anyone sane would have disbanded the House, sent them all away and turned the place into a series of storage closets.

Not Dumbledore. The adult reader is left wondering if he is suffering from a mental condition as well. Because if he's allowing this so that he can keep his eye on them, he's doing a poor job of it. Rowling Two, Annoying Critic Three.

In the second book, Harry experiences a great many "worst pains he has ever felt in his life." From encountering lethal fauna and flora to the battle in the Chamber of Secrets, Harry experiences enough trauma to send half a dozen youngsters to a trauma specialist. And by the end of the book Harry is beginning to show signs that he might need one.

But Rowling saves her real one-two punch to Harry's psyche for book three. First there are the Dementors, and Harry gets a taste of their particular brand of pleasantry early on.

There's a very interesting theme starting here: the adults you trust (parents) are not always able to save you. It's a subtle form of trauma that most modern real-world children don't actually encounter until they are much older than Harry's thirteen years, unless they have the misfortune to be the victims of abuse or disaster. The simple brush with such helplessness during the destruction of the World Trade Center, whether experienced live or on television, sent youngsters all over the country to counselors and therapists.

However, fictional (and real-world) adolescents of the past were sadly all too familiar with that helplessness. From the waifs laboring in "dark satanic mills" to the children of British expatriates sent "home" to the indifferent or cruel attentions of paid guardians or boarding schools, from Kipling to Kingsley, the books (and the world) were full of it. Rowling joins a very long line of authors in that tradition, and if fewer children these days are familiar with that world-shattering helplessness, nevertheless, fictional or as a reflection of reality, it's a viable theme.

161

Still. Harry does come in for more than his share of it.

And by book four, the poor lad ought to be a raving lunatic. The bloom is off the rose for poor Harry. No longer the darling of the wizarding world, no longer subject to contempt and persecution only at the hands of one House of his fellow students, by book four more adults than just Lord Voldemort and his Death Eaters have set their sights on him, and they lay down a barrage of withering fire.

Now in this case, Nitpicking Critic has to concede to Rowling. A great deal of this rings true, and even Harry's age doesn't negate it. All you have to do is pick up a supermarket tabloid to see the same sort being given to treatment of media child-stars. The wonder of it is that Harry hasn't got as many PTSD counselors on his payroll as young actors do. Rowling Three, Obnoxious Critic Three.

And this, of course, is the book where Harry gets the real kick between the eyes, because this is the book in which someone dies— is murdered, in fact—right in front of him. It has, of course, been said repeatedly that Lord Voldemort and the Death Eaters have killed people, but Harry has never seen it for himself.

Now here is where the Irritating Critic is divided. On the one hand, you could make the case that Harry ought to have been driven into some sort of mental state by the shock. But on the other hand, you could also point out that all of his angst up until this point has conditioned him to handle it. People have *almost* died in his presence, and those were his friends. It's not as if he really knows Cedric all that well. Still, one envisions years of therapy thanks to this, and at least one therapist's high-dollar sports car.

All of this is, of course, merely the warm-up for book five, which features a genuine sadist and the death of Harry's guardian and link to his dead parents, Sirius Black.

And book six—where Dumbledore himself is murdered.

And at this point Nattering Critic simply has to shut up, and presume that Harry is repressing all this. There's plenty of precedent for that in the real and fictional worlds, too. That's why it's called *Post-Traumatic Stress Disorder*.

Somewhere, out there in the fictional world of Harry Potter, there's a PTSD counselor avidly reading the wizarding papers, rubbing his hands and thinking happily of how he'll be able to pay the college fees for his kids once all of this comes back to haunt the Boy Who Lived.

In high school, MERCEDES LACKEY was the goalkeeper for the Highland Flingers Quidditch team, which held the record for the most consecutive losses of any team in the state of Indiana. This is partly explained by the fact that they were forced to practice at night with no lights to avoid the attention of the local Muggles.

She is the author of *The Fairy Godmother*, the Elemental Masters series, the Heralds of Valdemar series, the Diana Tregarde series and many others, all of which the Muggles seem to think are fantasies.

ROXANNE LONGSTREET CONRAD

The Proper Wizard's Guide to Good Manners

A M*ggle Tells All

A LIVELY EXCURSION INTO THE WIZARDING WORLD AND THE MIS-
CONCEPTIONS THEY HAVE ABOUT THE REST OF US, NOTABLE FOR
THE FIRST COGENT EXPLANATION I HAVE YET SEEN FOR THE SARTO-
RIAL ECCENTRICITIES OF WITCHES AND WIZARDS AMONGST US.

WHY, YOU MIGHT ASK, would it be necessary for a
Magically Challenged Person[1] such as myself (even one who has been taken into the gener-
ously padded bosom of the wizarding community)
to write about so seminal a work as *The Proper
Wizard's Guide to Conduct in the Non-Magical World*? After all, that
worthy volume has been haunting the shelves (in some cases, quite
literally) for more than thirty years and, in that time, has become
the bestselling work of advice in the history of the wizarding world.[2]
What could possibly be left to explore about such a well-known
work?

---

[1] A clarification of the term "Non-Wizard" or "Magically Challenged Person": In using these rather vague terms, I am of course following the recent message issued by the Ministry, as follows: "Due to recent unpleasant reactions from the public, we have taken steps to make our publications less 'wizard-centric.' The use of terms such as 'M*ggle' are deemed to be offensive and shall henceforth not be used in reference guides. We shall, instead, transform the term to 'non-wizard' to refer to those who are magically challenged. (This will occur automagically for all works already completed, published and bound.) Failure to comply with this request going forward will result in fines and administrative confinement."

[2] Source: *Books In Foolscap, Ed. 792.*

As we are about to see...everything.

While countless learned wizards have read and agreed with the conclusions of this important reference, as far as I can determine no one from the so-called "normal" world has ever cast a critical eye upon the contents. I picked it up at a used bookstore intending merely to glance at it...and was shocked to discover that there was plenty to question about *The Proper Wizard's Guide*. I had always found some of the wizarding world's ideas about non-magical society inexplicable...until they were revealed to me, page after page, by this important *and inaccurate* work.

It may be a fool's errand, but I'll attempt to set straight many of the long-cherished misconceptions—one non-wizard's attempt to reconcile the wizarding world with, well, everything else.

It is a daunting task. Naturally, I attempted to contact the esteemed author (Mistress Demelza Dunning, who also authored *What Not to Wear to a Christening* and *The Proper Wizard's Guide to Making Love...Potions*) through her publisher, Bother & Feathergill, and met with no success. My inquiry received the following reply, which I suspect was penned by Automatic Quill:

> Dear Sir or Madam:
> We thank you for your kind inquiry regarding our bestselling work, *The Proper Wizard's Guide to Conduct in the Non-Magical World*. Mistress Dunning is, as you know, very busy with new projects and cannot respond to your owl in person at this time. However, we enclose a chapbook of her latest work, *Owls and You: Making The Most of Your Postal System* as a thank-you gift.
> Sincerely,
>
> Frederick Feathergill IV
> Publisher

I find this sincerity a matter for deep suspicion, as the publication date on *Owls And You* was some twenty years ago, and Frederick Feathergill IV kicked off this mortal coil in 1985, but in short, my questions were met with, as it were, stony silence.

So I was forced to proceed on my own—with great trepidation, and with a suitable supply of firewhiskey (for fortitude) and chocolate (to counteract any negative psychological effects)—to address the most egregious misconceptions of *The Proper Wizard's Guide*. Without further ado....

THE PROPER WIZARD'S GUIDE
TO CONDUCT IN
THE NON-MAGICAL WORLD

By Demelza Dunning

presented by
Bother & Feathergill

publishers of fine volumes

Exception Alley

165

Opening to the Preface revealed this recommendation:

> Keep this handy reference guide with you at all times, disguised as a non-magical map. (Please take note that non-magical maps do not move, change or correct you when you wander off your specified path. I know, it's terrifically annoying, but we must all make sacrifices.)

Sage advice. I certainly have nothing to dispute in that declaration. Most wizards I've spoken with are amazed at the idea that "regular" maps not only don't move, but must be reprinted in order to show important revisions. (As you know, wizarding maps are simply hexed into order. A much more sensible system; I've often wished I could do the same to my tattered road guides.)

So the Preface, at least, contained nothing objectionable.

However, turning the page to chapter one, "Proper Attire in the

Non-Magical World," opened up a whole new vista of odd—and sometimes dangerous—misconceptions.

Despite my long-standing acquaintance with the wizarding world, I have spent much of my life puzzling over the bizarre conventions that govern wizard fashion. It seems to have stopped dead in its tracks—for all but the youngest—sometime in the early twentieth century, and unlike non-magical fashions—which come and go in waves—wizard fashions tend to...linger.

And here, in the pages of this most unlikely source, I discovered the reason not only for the odd confabulation of fashions in the wizarding world, but also their myopic insistence on wearing odd clothing on their visits to more modern environs.

Even more disturbingly, *it all made sense.*

It is common knowledge that the wearing of traditional dress—from whatever period of wizarding history you prefer—has a strengthening effect upon the powers of the modern witch or wizard. This time-honored connection to our revered—and more powerful—ancestors is no doubt both prudent and stylish.

This revealed a far more logical landscape to me, in terms of wizarding fashion. The witch on the corner, who favors a dusty Edwardian–style matron's dress? Her most powerful grand-ancestor no doubt came into the fullness of her powers in that particular period. It does make one wonder why no one has continued the tradition on into more modern times—no one favors, for instance, the Leisure Suit, although there were certainly some prodigiously powerful wizards around while it was in fashion—but upon reflection, it seems to me that the more modern historical periods NOT represented in wizarding dress all date to around, or after, the appearance of...*He-Who-Shall-Not-Be-Named.*

Which brings us to the question of "fitting in."

Sadly, the wearing of traditional dress creates a vague sense of unease among non-wizards unless they are provided with some sensible reason for not following current ephemeral trends. But fear not! I have spent some time among this population, absorbing their ways and culture, and I have formulated strategies that will allow you to retain your wizarding world charm and sartorial dignity while sinking seamlessly "below the Ray Darr," as the locals say. (I have inquired as to the identity of Mr. Darr, but no one seems to know.)

- OPTION 1: *The eccentric vagabond.* If you wish to wear your wizard robes, use your oldest possible, obtain some sort of push-cart and mumble to yourself while perambulating the streets. You are unlikely to be accosted. The great advantage of this disguise is that you may, if asked, freely admit to being a wizard. No one will believe you. You might even collect spare coins from passersby to pay for the bus or train, if you are particularly effective.
- OPTION 2: *I'm in a play.* Period clothing is entirely believable so long as you claim to be on your way to a production of a classic theatrical play. However, this approach often leads to questions regarding the name of the play, the location of the theater and whether or not you can secure free tickets to the event. Use with caution.
- OPTION 3: *Historical recreations and festivals.* No matter whether you are prone to medieval skirts or Victorian top hats, capes or frock coats, this excuse will carry you safely through any question, so long as you mention that the festival is "outside of town," and "very boring."

In casting my mind back, I can think of several witches and wizards who have followed this scarily apropos advice. Most adopt the "eccentric vagabond" approach, as I recall. It is indeed terrifyingly effective at deflecting attention. It also makes me wonder about the grimy man I passed last night on the way to the take-away stand, who tried to tell me about satellites reading my brain waves from orbit. Most unsettling.

However accurate her instructions on fitting in might be, her special urgings to younger witches are less so:

For the svelte, young witch desiring to fit seamlessly into a proper non-magical setting, we recommend the acquisition of mini skirts—the shorter the better—which should be worn without leggings of any kind, and with the addition of very tall shoes. This is considered very modest and maidenly attire, and should be appropriate for any occasion.[3]

I found this advice, in hindsight, questionable. Taking a bit of initiative I felt necessary for the sake of accuracy, I owled the author directly[4] and asked about the source of this particular bit of wisdom.

I received a violently loud message in return, by Express Owl. I shall paraphrase it to say that at no time did Mistress Dunning truly recommend that young witches dress, in her colorful terms, "like pavement nymphs." Apparently Master Feathergill, before his untimely kicking off, exercised an editorial prerogative to express his own opinion.

168

Naturally, since accessories make the outfit, these tiresome restrictions can be livened up with the addition of traditional accessories, such as dramatic layers of scarves, amusingly enchanted stickpins or—of course—the current chapeau trend toward Ever-Changing Slogan caps.

I shudder to think how many otherwise bright witches and wizards have draped themselves in yards and yards of multicolored yarn scarves to gad about London based upon this questionable advice.[5]

As to the amusingly enchanted stickpins, the legendarily unfortunate incident with Master Thesper's accessories singing a bawdy version of "God Save The Queen (He Might Be Hungry Later)" at

---

[3] From a Reader Owl saved from the publisher's rubbish bin by a disgruntled former employee: "Dear Mistress Dunning: Your fashion advice was FANTASTIC! My mum was none too pleased when I put on the skin-tight six-inch micro mini skirt and the four-inch heels, but you would simply not believe what a smash I was with the lads. Some of them wanted to give me the funny currency they use in London to take a walk with them—couldn't make any sense out of it, but it was a laugh and a half. Mum says I'm not allowed out again until I turn thirty-five, when my hips will be too big to wear that sort of thing. Could you please owl her and tell her that it's all in fun? Sincerely, Bethesda Brightwell." No record of any response from Mistress Dunning. Not that I particularly blame her.

[4] Rumors concerning my blackmailing of Mistress Dunning's agent (whose wife might not appreciate his visit to the giantess-run brothel as much as the pictures indicate he did) for the proper address should be disregarded. Not that I've seen any such pictures. Or know of any such establishment.

[5] Although I can, of course, think of one in particular, who called himself The Doctor. Changeable sort. I suspect he might have been a Metamorphmagus, although he was rather firm on the idea of not wanting anything to do with Ministry affairs.

a state dinner must serve as a clear indication of how dangerous this advice can be. It might have been the only recorded instance in which a Coldstream Guard was heard to exclaim "Blimey!" while on duty.

Oddly, Mistress Dunning's further advice seems either quite prescient, or demonstrates the persistence of bad taste. For instance:

> For the more matronly witch, and for wizards of all ages, we recommend "shorts." You may match these with any top, short or long sleeved, which in your estimation is of sharply contrasting (or clashing) color and fabric, and is preferably emblazoned with your national flag of origin. Also, "Earth Shoes" are a welcome addition to any outfit.

Walk around London and you'll see that, sadly, this advice really is timeless.

With my heart in my throat (subsequently washed back down to its proper place by a fortifying drink of firewhiskey) I moved on to chapter two: "Places to Visit." Luckily, this was less stressful, requiring only a few pieces of chocolate to ease the pain of Mistress Dunning's eggplant-shaded prose. (Four pieces to be exact and, yes, one rather large tumbler of the aforementioned firewhiskey. I had to wash it down, didn't I?)

169

This section is still largely accurate, including the lovely fairy–style "House in the Clouds" in Thorpeness, Suffolk, and the giant pineapple house in Dunmore, near Sterling. And Mistress Dunning is quite correct to point out that no wizard should venture near Exmouth without visiting the circular house—specially built to deprive evil spirits of corners in which to hide. I haven't personally visited these legendary vacation destinations, but I understand they are popular with my non-magical relatives as well. Mistress Dunning also quite properly recommends visits to Madame Tussaud's of London, and sternly cautions against the temptation to hex any of the wax figures into lifelike motion—which, while most amusing, is off-putting for most other visitors.

Chapter three is entitled "Using Non-Magical Speech in Social Settings," and there was thankfully nothing immediately dangerous in what I reviewed, which included some quite handy information for those not accustomed to life in the non-magical community, such as:

> It is important that in casual conversation with non-magical folk you avoid any mention of the following: spells, hexes, witches, wizards, witchcraft, magic, flying (other than in M*ggle aeroplanes), the Ministry, owl post or centaurs. You may, however, mention vampires (they are all the cultural rage), werewolves (non-magical folk have a startlingly good grasp of this topic) and giants (although only in North America, as it is the proper name of some sort of sports organization, I understand).

Here, however, Mistress Dunning's advice becomes somewhat questionable:

170

> A safe topic of conversation in nearly every circumstance would be to discuss sporting events. Generally, most of these types of conversations tend to evolve toward two diametrically opposite positions; therefore, it is advisable to simply adopt the negative of whatever your conversational companion might say. For instance, if he says: "What did you think of the last Arsenals match?" you should immediately respond, "Bollocks! What a bunch of punters!" This will ensure you a long and lively dialogue.[6]

Technically true, yes. But an approach best restricted to situations in which you are confident in your ability to, if not best your conversational partner in a fair fight, at least outrun them. Later in the chapter, buried deep, there was also this bit of dubious wisdom:

> It can be quite difficult to shed the habits of a lifetime in casual conversation. Accordingly, I urge you to familiarize yourself with things that

---

[6] From another Reader Owl: "Dear Mistress Dunning: I regret to inform you that although I certainly did my best, my attempt to strike up a conversation in a local public house was less than successful when following your advice. By 'unsuccessful' I mean, of course, 'bloody awful,' in that I was attacked by all inhabitants of the pub, including the barman, the barmaid, two barristers and a Church of England cleric. I was, of course, able to hold my own against the barristers, the barman and the barmaid, but the C of E cleric fair kicked the shite out of me. I respectfully request you revise this area of your very fine work to avoid such confrontations in the future. Sincerely yours, Caddog Cantington." Unfortunately, Mistress Dunning seems not to have heeded his advice.

are all the rage in non-magical society these days, such as moving pictures (which, despite the name, are not enchanted, but simply a rather clumsy series of images flickered rapidly, one after another) and television (a mystifying alteration of the former, which requires the use of a receiving set, snack foods and a sad lowering of one's literary standards).

Some examples of moving pictures one might appropriately discuss: *Valley of the Dolls*, an inoffensive children's film about winsome magically animated toys, and *Lolita*, which I am told is a biographical account of the famous Lolita Lovegood Lindy, a witch who successfully masqueraded as a famous opera singer (and rarely resorted to a magically amplified voice).

If you are forced to discuss television, simply say that you quite enjoyed the televised walking tour of Hollywood, appropriately named *Star Trek*.

Oh, dear. If there is any area of non-wizarding society in which one cannot make mistakes like these, it is in popular culture. I owled Mistress Dunning urging her to correct this information (I was unable to resist, despite her previous response). The result was a quite rude reply telling me to "naff off." I remain unclear as to whether she was demonstrating her command of colorful non-magical colloquial expression, detailed on page forty-three, or had got the wind up about my barrage of feathered communiqués. Probably the latter.

After a pause to refresh my glass—two or three times (one can never have too much fortitude, you know)—and emptying half a box of fine Belgian chocolates (really, quite extraordinary), I turned to chapter four, "Common Non-Magical Items You May Encounter."

This proved to be a curious mixture of the logical and the peculiarly fanciful. For instance, Mistress Dunning quite rightly declares:

> While most wizards have, of course, experienced bus transit, you should be aware that unlike magical conveyances, non-magical buses operate upon widely published schedules and cannot be summoned upon requirement (or at least, not without attracting considerable notice).

Her advice on Tube transportation is similarly—and refreshing-ly—direct and accurate, although I can't really imagine how she could misinterpret the Tube system, as even the dimmest wizard has been seen to successfully navigate it with only a few unfortunate side trips.

However, she begins to wander into less sanguine territory on the subject of taxicabs:

> Taxis are another method of transit available in most cities, and may be summoned by a piercing ululating shriek, not unlike that of a Dementor, followed by throwing oneself on the hood of the speed-ing vehicle.

This might very well explain the continued steady stream of patients arriving at St. Mungo's with descriptions of having been "run down like they were invisible."

My repeated owls to Mistress Dunning were returning, by this point, empty-clawed and looking rather wide of eye (even for owls), so I was unable to determine the source of this rather interesting piece of advice.

Happily, the author is correct in her description of telephones:

> Telephones are found in almost all buildings. They allow non-wiz-ards to communicate over long distances with one another, but only voice communication. Naturally, this system is clumsy and off-put-ting, but you simply must learn to adapt to its odd behaviors. For instance, in order to speak, you must *lift the handset* and *hold it to your ear*. You will find, in this position, that the end bit fits rather conveniently near your mouth, requiring only a minor adjustment in order to speak.
>
> One word of caution: this "technology" is primitive, at best, and therefore you should speak clearly and loudly at all times. You should also follow the end of each declarative sentence with the designation, "OVER" which allows the listener on the other end to understand that you are now finished speaking.

Well...she's at least got it nearly right. And it certainly explains the loud, clumsy conversations I've held with my wizarding friends via telephone.

However:

> I have been reliably informed that if the tethering wires are inconvenient, a "wireless phone" can be created from any phone tethered to the wall simply by pulling it free with a brisk tug. This seems to be utterly sensible and yet—bafflingly enough—fails to work upon field testing. I understand that there are working "wireless phones" in the non-magical world, although what adjustment is required when yanking free the wires in order to create one is unclear.

At this point, I ran out of firewhiskey and was forced to nip down to the shop. No firewhiskey being available, I settled for blended Scotch, and stocked up on two additional boxes of chocolates. Just in case.

Luckily, Mistress Dunning was somewhat more insightful on the subject of other M*ggle communication channels:

> You will not find owl post a common sight in travels beyond our borders—instead, mailboxes serve as the non-wizarding equivalent. A letter must be fully and properly addressed in order to find its way to the right person. Simply writing "Imelda Betterman-Inslow, Harrow House, The Bottoms" will not ensure its proper arrival. And do not neglect to affix postage to the missive. Postage consists of small squares of colored paper, glued to the envelope, which feature non-moving pictures of generally deceased individuals, with a valuation. One does wonder why the Queen is only valued at 10p, however. It seems disrespectful. Also, curiously, she is not deceased.

Mistress Dunning remains thankfully silent on more modern inventions such as the Internet and e-mail. I don't think there could be enough firewhiskey in the world, frankly.

In tipsily surveying the book, at this point I discovered that I was moving close to the end—a blessing for you as well as me, I'm certain. Having fortified myself sufficiently, I moved on to chapter five, "What M*ggles Know About Magic."

Magic is something that is both common to the non-magical world, and entirely discounted. There are vast wastelands of so-called fantasy novels with misleading information on the use—and abuse—of magic in all its forms. Luckily, these books are so far afield from actual spellcraft that they pose no threat—and, of course, non-wizards find them the subject of mere amusement, rather than instruction manuals.

Books such as *The Witch's Bible* and *The Necronomicon*, while popular among the faux-witch set, contain next to no useful information on how to go about practical hexing and curses, much less decent potion-making. Occasionally, a non-magical person will catch a glimpse of something that should not be seen, and for their own good, the Ministry will assist them in forgetting that traumatic experience. The few who escape this effort are no doubt responsible for the garbled accounts of ghosts, UFOs and governmental conspiracies that dominate the popular non-magical tabloid press.

174

I—and no doubt the grimy man on the way to the Indian takeaway stand—disagree with her about the governmental conspiracies, which any person of sense must admit seem credible. And I disagreed with her a lot more (or at least a lot more vigorously) after two fingers of Scotch.

While we are on the subject of non-magical works of fiction, one area of the non-magical literary emporium that I find thoroughly reliable is the section entitled *Romance*, which contains colorfully written information on non-magical courtship and dating practices. I perused one entitled *Enchanted Embrace*, which seemed most likely to appeal to the wizarding sensibility (at least by title). Most witches to whom I subsequently offered it seemed to rather enjoy it, and at least three were steadfast in their assertion that "our society would be vastly improved if wizards bothered to learn a thing or two about women."

The wizards to whom I loaned the volume harrumphed loudly and professed a violent dislike for the material, although upon detailed questioning, most admitted to having re-read pages 237 through 245...several times.

Imagine my shock at discovering that I also have a copy of *Enchanted Embrace* sitting on my bookshelves...and yes, I've leafed through to page 237 more than once...so perhaps the non-magical and wizarding communities are not as different as a volume such as *The Proper Wizard's Guide* would lead one to believe. We are clearly united in our pursuit of love, romance, and...ah, literature. However, the words "thoroughly reliable" in this section do make one shudder, just a bit.

(After retrieving the volume and reading it aloud to my screech owl Lucifer, complete with flinging myself about in a very entertaining demonstration of the excesses of pages 237 to 245, I downed another shot of Scotch and fell asleep on the floor, after playing a CD of Berlioz's *Symphonie Fantastique* at thunderingly loud levels while conducting with my roommate's borrowed wand. Seemed like the thing to do.)

175

In the morning, which arrived far too bright and hideously too early, I skimmed the end of the book as I finished the chocolate for breakfast. (Chocolate, it seems, is nearly as restorative in the case of hangovers as in that of Dementors.) Mistress Dunning brings her groundbreaking work to a close with a flashy, much-admired section, which for thirty years has been seen as the definitive work on the subject of "M*ggle Dating Conventions."

It's no wonder that marriages between the two worlds are looked down on in the wizarding community, given the state of her advice—the wonder is that any of them actually succeed at all. To wit:

As I have determined through research and field study of moving picture presentations, the typical "first date" in non-magical society goes something like this: One of the parties—usually the gentleman—will dress in a tradesman's uniform, preferably as a plumber, television repairman or police officer. This usually involves a tight-fitting pair of trousers and a large, rather clumsy tool belt. The lady will answer the door wearing a thin—preferably transparent—garment, or at least an unbelted robe. At some point, she will inquire whether or not the gentleman has a screwdriver in his pocket. From this point, events become rapidly more energetic, and we will draw a veil of modesty over the proceedings.

One should certainly be prepared for this, if dating a non-magical person. It is only polite to follow the customs.

The last owl inquiry I dispatched to Mistress Dunning returned hexed into a small flying pig, and I had the very devil of a time convincing my roommate to transform the poor creature back to its usual state, but it did carry a reply, as follows:

Dear Pest:

I resent the implication that I failed to accurately research the subject! Why, I consulted the foremost expert on the subject of Non-Magical Courtship and Morality, Professor Onan Orwell, who not only provided the research material, but assured me that so-called "blue movies" are completely factual in their depiction of non-magical interpersonal relations. (I will admit to some puzzlement that they are, in fact, not "blue" at all, but are depicted in full and living color.) But I stand by my conclusions in this, as in every part of *The Proper Wizard's Guide*. I am quite sure that many wizards and witches have engaged in very satisfactory first dates while utilizing my advice.

—DD

However adamant her defense, I'm the one living in the non-magical world (even with a witch for a roommate), and my conclusion must be that willy-nilly home repair is not advisable for first dates. Anywhere.

Mistress Dunning's concluding few paragraphs contained nothing of note, as with most concluding paragraphs, although they warned once again against the dangers of discussing magical subjects within earshot of non-magical persons, something that even with a splitting hangover I can't fault. Not without more chocolate, anyway.

I was just about to put the book aside when I turned one final page, to discover this:

I call upon the publishers for two things. First, an updated edition of *The Proper Wizard's Guide,* which will hopefully address the shortcomings I have pointed out in these pages. And second, the banning of the underhanded use of a covert advertisement, since obviously there is an embedded spell attached to this last page—I found myself out in the bookstore again within the hour, still wearing my slippers (although thankfully otherwise fully dressed) and searching the shelves frantically for this book. Unable to locate it, I settled for buying every other book in Ms. Winglesham's oeuvre.

Insidious spell.

Now, if you'll excuse me, I feel a compulsion to read....

ROXANNE LONGSTREET CONRAD is a worrisome confabulation of persons, including Rachel Caine, Julie Fortune, Roxanne Longstreet, Roxanne Conrad and Ian Hammell (she has no idea what Ian writes, actually, and that's probably for the best). She has Web sites, the most prominent of which is www.rachelcaine.com.

Until recently, she was a recovering Harry Potter addict. Sadly, the recovery process ground to a halt after she was discovered gazing dreamily at her lenticular Sirius Black wanted poster and her autographed photo of Snape while holding her Hermione Granger wand and wearing her Time-Turner pendant.

She also was honored by being appointed Head of Slytherin House at *The Witching Hour*, a 2005 Harry Potter symposium in Salem, Massachusetts. Blackmail photos abound.

Why Killing Harry Is the Worst Outcome for Voldemort

AS KIPLING POINTED OUT, "THE FEMALE OF THE SPECIES IS MORE DEADLY THAN THE MALE." APPLYING THIS ASSERTION TO THE WORLD OF HARRY POTTER, RICHARD GARFINKLE OUTLINES THE RESULTING CAMPAIGN SHOULD VOLDEMORT MAKE THE MISTAKE OF TRULY MAKING HERMIONE GRANGER ANGRY.

THUS SPAKE THE SYBIL, Trelawney, unto the great Wizard Dumbledore:

The one with the power to vanquish the Dark Lord approaches.... Born to those who have thrice defied him, born as the seventh month dies.... And the Dark Lord will mark him as his equal, but he will have power the Dark Lord knows not.... And either must die at the hand of the other for neither can live while the other survives.... The one with the power to vanquish the Dark Lord will be born as the seventh month dies....

Let us consider what happens if, when the prophesied day comes, things do not go as expected. Suppose Voldemort and Harry Potter face each other for the last time, wand against wand, spell against spell. We expect that Harry will emerge victorious—battered perhaps, but still the survivor.

But what happens if it is the Dark Lord who triumphs? If upon that hour Lord Voldemort stands above the lifeless corpse of the Boy Who Lived. If, accompanied by the happy cackles of his Death Eaters, he gloats his triumph to the world, crowing forth mockery against prophecy and hope, crying doom, doom, doom to the wizard and Muggle worlds.

From that moment Voldemort is royally hosed. It is his own doom that he shouts. For the moment Harry dies is the moment when the most dangerous person in the Potterverse becomes Voldemort's true and final enemy. He will face no longer the power of Harry Potter, but the more terrible force—the brain of Hermione Granger.

Let's face it: Harry may be powerful and brave, but he is at heart a jock and a slacker. I will leave to the more psychologically minded the question of whether being raised by abusive Muggles is responsible for these two characteristics, and to the more conspiracy-minded the deeper question of whether Dumbledore had him raised by those selfsame Muggles because he wanted Harry to be a jock and a slacker. Instead, let us look at how these two characteristics have made Harry a weak opponent for a dangerous all-rounder like Voldemort.

Harry's sole magical gifts are in Quidditch and Defense Against the Dark Arts. Both have served him well in his conflicts with the Dark Lord, but as is seen in *Harry Potter and the Order of the Phoenix*, Harry is susceptible to having his mind messed with. He lacks the skills to defend himself against this, and he has been too much of a slacker to stick with the training he needs to overcome that deficiency.

Even if he had put in the work necessary to defend against mental attack, Harry is still susceptible to the jockish tendency toward senseless heroism. Voldemort waved a red flag, Harry charged at it and Sirius died.

Who was it who foresaw the danger and warned Harry that Voldemort was manipulating him? Not a prophet, not a seer of the future, but Hermione. Hermione saw through Voldemort's plans as though they were graven on glass. She, unlike Harry, would not have fallen into the trap at the Ministry. She reluctantly went along on that ill-fated expedition for two reasons: friendship and her long-standing tendency toward bowing to authority, even if the authority is Harry.

Knee-jerk obedience has kept Hermione in the shadows. She assumes, until it is proven otherwise, that those in power know what they are doing—a sad blind spot, and an amazing one, for someone who grew up in modern Muggledom. Fortunately, as the story has progressed, Hermione has begun to break out of this shell. In the early books she would only defy those in power for friendship's sake, but in *Order of the Phoenix* Hermione instigated the covert Defense Against the Dark Arts classes and picked Harry as the teacher, knowing talent when she saw it. The shell has begun to crack, though it would take a greater shock to shatter it.

What happens to Hermione on the day Harry Potter dies?

On that day the last of her illusions, her faith in Dumbledore, would likely disappear. For some people this would betoken a turning toward evil, but not Hermione. For her, disillusionment would be the breaking of her chrysalis, the emergence of the great and terrible witch within her—great and terrible not because of her power, which is considerable, but because she thinks, plans and is careful. No one else in the Potterverse, neither wizard nor Muggle, does all three.

181

What would Hermione do if Harry died? Would she charge up to attack Voldemort, seeking to vent her grief in a senseless act of suicide?

Don't be daft. Harry would be dead. Voldemort would have triumphed. She wouldn't be able to do anything about that immediately. Hermione, as so far depicted, is just not strong enough to fight Voldemort. Even if she had the power, the prophecy would stand in her way. She could not vanquish the Dark Lord.

What would she do? Probably she would exercise common sense where no one else had.

She would grab Ron, who would naturally be there, and she would run away. First, she would Disapparate to some distant place. Then, there, it is likely that Hermione would do what Hermione does best. She would study.

It's unlikely that she would be alone. There are some people Hermione could not leave behind unless she had no choice. First on this list would be Ron, because the two of them are so obviously in love it makes you want to hit them over the head with a mallet and shout, "Get a room!"

Along with Ron she would likely take Neville, out of friendship, and because he has started to show potential, and Ginny, because she knows the inside of Voldemort's mind. If her common sense outweighed the last shreds of her old views, Hermione would also take the Weasley twins. Any insurgency she would raise against Voldemort would need weapons manufacturers and low-down, sneaky, dirty, underhanded tacticians and commandoes. Fred and George are all of these and much more.

Probably the most difficult choice that would face the girl under these circumstances would be whether or not to return and fight alongside the Order of the Phoenix. Tempting though it would be, that way lies nothing more than a hero's death—because the Order of the Phoenix will lose. She could try to rescue Molly and Arthur Weasley, or Professor McGonagall, or Hagrid or the older Weasley boys

or Lupin or any of the others, but doing so would bring Voldemort down on her head. And she would know, as Harry refused to know, that she is not ready to fight the Dark Lord.

She would have to leave the Order of the Phoenix to fight their last battles, knowing that they would want her and her charges to be safe and ready to rise again from their ashes when the time is right.

Where would she go?

Away from England, for a start. She would take her parents and hide them. They might be targets for petty revenge, but as Muggles they would not be worth Voldemort's—or that of any Death Eater's—efforts to find. This is the Dark Lord's blind spot, one that will serve to keep her safe for the time she needs to prepare: in Voldemort's eyes she and her fellows would not be worth the effort. The only person associated with Voldemort who might want personal revenge on her and Ron is Draco, but he is more likely to spend his time kissing up.

Where would she go?

Anywhere she could learn. Hermione has shown that she knows her capacities and her limitations, unlike Harry. Under these circumstances she, who had always been a follower, would have to learn to lead. She would need lessons in generalship, in creating a guerrilla army, in fighting against established and overwhelming power. In the Potterverse such lessons are easily available. She could read books (Muggle and wizard) and talk to ghosts. She could even interrogate portraits of great military wizards. Over time she would study magic, tactics and strategy, how to run an insurgent organization, how to start a whispering campaign, and how to undermine those in power.

Hermione would—given her tenderheartedness—obviously regret what she had to leave behind. Voldemort in power would make a terror of England. Even so, she would know that it was nowhere near as bad as it could be.

To see why, let's look at Voldemort for a moment:

In personality he is a petty tyrant, interested in flashy exercise and the showing off of power, not in the systematic repression of a truly dangerous dictator. And the Death Eaters, while powerful, are in personality fawning slaves. None of them, from Lucius Malfoy on down to the pettiest, has any real ability beyond their powers, or any ambition beyond that of the schoolyard bully. Hermione, I think, would understand what Harry should have: that the Death Eaters one and all are just a bunch of jumped-up Dudley Dursleys.

Schoolyard bullies never need to go looking for targets. Out of sight, out of mind, out of range. Hermione could arrange to be all three of these. That would leave plenty of people for the bullies to torment. Ugly as the situation would be, Hermione would have to sacrifice those people in order to have time to learn and to create the organization that would fight back and ultimately free them.

In forming such a group, Hermione's greatest advantage would come out of Voldemort's contempt for Muggles. She was born and raised among Muggles. She learned to live as a Muggle before she ever knew there was such a thing as magic, before she dreamed of being a witch. Hermione Granger sees both sides of the world, magical and Muggle, and sees the strengths and weaknesses of both. Wizards see Muggle technology as attempts to imitate magic, so they ignore it—except for connoisseurs like Arthur Weasley, and even his understanding is extraordinarily limited. The Death Eaters themselves are blind to the advantages of modern Muggledom.

183

Hermione, steeped in this understanding, could do with her budding organization what no Muggle group could get away with: she could hand laptops to her followers and e-mail them instructions. No wizard would dream of looking on the Internet for enemies.

To build such an organization, funds would be essential. Financing her freedom fighters would be surprisingly simple thanks to two factors: the vulnerability of Muggle markets (stock, art, commodities) to magical manipulation, and Gringotts' ability to exchange Muggle money for wizard coins. It seems clear that the only thing preventing wizards from using Muggles to make a fortune is the Ministry of Magic, and with Voldemort in power the Ministry would be shut down. (All of which makes one wonder: are those goblins doing this kind of thing already? Are they responsible for the state of modern finance? Nah, it takes humans to be that silly.)

Time is the other thing Hermione would need as much of as possible. Fortunately she has had experience tinkering with it. It is likely that before leaving England, in the midst of the chaos of Voldemort's rise, Hermione would swipe a Time-Turner or two from the Ministry.[1] Using them she could gain much in the way of learning at the cost of confusion and aging, acceptable losses to someone who has seen her dearest friend die and has vowed revenge.

It may sound unlikely that Hermione would take these cold-blooded actions, for she is a young woman of scruples as well as brains. But in the matter of Rita Skeeter, Hermione Granger showed that she would abandon a great many moral objections for the sake of revenge. And in the luring of Professor Umbridge toward the centaurs she showed a willingness to manipulate others for what she sees as good ends.

Even with a Time-Turner Hermione would require several years in which to learn all she needed. In that time she would have to hold the other young people together against their own impatience. But she can be forceful. Ron, Neville and Ginny would bend to her views, they too having seen Harry's folly. She would likely set them

---

[1] Though the original supply housed at the Ministry is reported to have been destroyed in the fight at the end of *Harry Potter and the Order of the Phoenix*, it is quite likely that more would have been found and relocated between that point and Harry's final battle with Voldemort.

researching, instructing them and directing their practices toward a broad range of magical and Muggle learnings.

The twins would be a different matter. It would be sensible to let them create as they see fit, since genius must be given room to create madness. The only thing Hermione would insist on would be that they learn how Muggles accomplish some of their dirty tricks, so that in the fearsome fertile ground of their minds Fred and George could bring together both worlds in the service of merciless practical jokes. Fred and George let loose to buy toys on the Internet and then enchant them? Shudder.

Hermione would need perhaps ten years to mature in her mind, her magic and her plans. Then, when the time was right, when she and her followers were prepared, she would...

...certainly not charge forth in blind heroic attack against Voldemort's entrenched power. Nonsense. She would strike, but in ways that Voldemort, in his arrogance, would not even notice. Like a sapper against a castle, Hermione would undermine Voldemort shovel by shovel.

185

Where is the most vulnerable point to attack the Death Eaters? We can presume that Hermione, schooled in strategy, would seek to find it. The Death Eaters have many blind spots, one of which Hermione has already shown a keen and angry interest in: the spells that bind house-elves to their masters. These spells would be one of her highest priorities, for all Death Eaters have house-elves. If she could (and she very likely could) reverse-engineer these spells, she could change them, affecting the loyalty and removing the bonds that constrain the fearsome magics of those dangerous little servants. The Society for the Protection of Elvish Welfare would emerge once more.

Here we come to another one of those ugly choices. Hermione could free the house-elves, but Kreacher has shown that loyalty can exist even in these slaves. I think she would choose not to free them, not yet. She would instead bind them anew so that she would be the master of the Death Eaters' house-elves. No longer would the SPEW be a civil rights organization. Now it would become a spy ring and assassins' group, planted in the hearths of Voldemort's followers.

At this point any number of courses of action would be open to Hermione. Some are more likely than others, based on her personality, the personalities of the Death Eaters and the available methods of insurgency and infiltration that she would have learned.

The Death Eaters' troubles would begin slowly. House-elves would be overheard talking about what they had heard from other house-elves about the other elves' masters plotting against their masters. There would be whisperings of concern for the safety of their beloved masters and mistresses. Objects would disappear from one Death Eater's home and be found in another. Gradually, throughout the wizarding world rumors would arise that, now that they were on top, the Death Eaters were turning against each other.

Then would commence the spells and curses and poisonings and other little potion effects so easily smuggled into homes. Death Eaters would begin to die. Voldemort's followers, having lived so long in mutual mistrust, would turn against each other and begin to do their own killing. Voldemort under these circumstances would find himself as a king with a court full of intrigue. Like many a monarch before him he would be distracted from ruling his domain.

 186

Caught in this web of betrayals, the Death Eaters would begin dueling with one another behind Voldemort's back. But the wands they would use in those duels would have been swapped for Fred and George's now lethal fake wands, wands that Apparate large amounts of explosives into the middle of these fights. Death Eater homes might explode, or be filled with poison gas or Muggle hallucinogens that produce amusingly lethal side effects when combined with the three Unforgivable Curses. These and other "practical jokes" would ensure a high fatality rate among the Death Eaters, Weasleys' Wizard Wheezes at their most effective.

Hermione would not likely be satisfied with thinning the ranks. After all, toady wizards are easy enough to replace. It would be necessary to strike against Voldemort himself. Hermione would no doubt create a careful plan. Here is one such possibility that uses many of the resources already demonstrated to exist in the Potterverse. It is not a simple plan, but it is well within Hermione's abilities.

When the ranks of their enemies are thinned enough, Hermione would begin the next and riskiest, but most vital, phase of her work. First, she would secretly place certain enchantments copied from

Hogwarts and other places upon the Riddle House, a place Voldemort would avoid in his triumph, but which, as we are shown in *Harry Potter and the Goblet of Fire*, he sees as a refuge when he needs one.

The house prepared, Hermione would then send out Ron and Neville as a team. She would have had the pair of them training for the past ten years until they could fight and spell as well as anyone. Ron would probably chafe under Hermione's teaching, but, having seen Harry fall from over-quick action, he would accept her love and judgment. Ron would know that Hermione's plans would give him the best chance to take revenge for Harry and his own parents.

Ron and Neville would undertake a few choice, visible actions against Voldemort's forces. Lucius and Draco Malfoy would both be killed directly and forcefully, as would other Death Eaters who had troubled Harry while he lived. The deaths of Crabbe and Goyle both senior and junior would show Voldemort that vengeance for Harry was in the offing.

Ron might not at first be recognized by the survivors of his attacks because Hermione would have him wear a turban and seem to be talking to himself, or to some half-audible voice. Neville would be seen and recognized but would appear to have only one hand. During this time, Voldemort would hear rumors of dead unicorns being found in various enchanted forests.

At last the house-elves would whisper, "The Boy Who Lived lives again."

Voldemort would fret, more so when he heard that one of the places where Ron and Neville were spotted was James Potter's grave. Afterwards the grave would be found to have been dug up and one arm bone taken, an act of desecration perhaps hard to credit to Hermione. But consider: would not James Potter have given his Marauder's blessing for this combination revenge and practical joke?

If things go according to plan, Voldemort's fretting would grow into full worry:

> *Bone of the father, unknowingly given, you will renew your son.*
> *Flesh of the servant, willingly given, you will revive your master.*
> *Blood of the enemy, forcibly taken, you will resurrect your foe.*

187

Voldemort would now be twitching on his throne, a fragile and tottering king. The first time they fought, Voldemort gave the baby Harry Potter much of his power. Could it be that when he seemed to kill Harry, seemed to triumph at last, all he had done was replay the past? Had he merely reduced the Boy Who Lived to that same condition he himself had suffered under for some eleven years before he emerged (and has it not been some eleven years since the boy wizard's death)? Was Harry Potter coming back? Back for the blood of the enemy and his own resurrection?

Seeking to prevent this, Voldemort would of course attack. Such forces as he has left, led by himself, would go hunting Ron and Neville. But they would not be found. Hermione would have had ten years (plus the time she gained using the Time-Turner), of research and application, and she would be dedicated in her studies.

Here we come to a question. Who is the more dangerous magician: Hermione trained as above, or Voldemort? I think that he would be no match for her in conventional magics—he relies too much upon the Unforgivable in his battles—and of course he cannot touch her in Muggle knowledge. Even if he can outwizard her, Voldemort would be no match for the twins in unconventional warfare after the decade of chaos they would have put under the belts, their genius fully loosed.

Let Voldemort hunt. He would find only smoke, and the whispers of Harry Potter's passage.

While he hunted, Hermione and her forces would undermine what remained of his power base, creating cells of rebel wizards and witches and arming them with Fred and George's creations. Using standard tactics for such groups they could rise up, attack and vanish again, not as wizards vanish, but into simple Muggle obscurity. Voldemort would hear that he had lost control, that some terrorist group called, variously, "Potter's Army," "Dumbledore's Army" or the "Third Order of the Phoenix," had risen to liberate England. And always he would hear the rallying cry: "For the Boy Who Lived!"

Voldemort isn't completely stupid. He would know that he was being baited. But who would he think was baiting him? Where Harry suffered from a hero complex, Voldemort suffers from acute villainy.

He would believe that Harry Potter was seeking to lure him back so that the ritual of flesh, blood and bone could be completed. But he is the Dark Lord. (Dramatic tone of voice) He Will Not Run.

Yet, he might muse, perhaps it would be wise not to confront Potter's Army directly. Yes. That would be better. He will reconstitute his forces first. But where to go?

And here Voldemort's instincts would betray him, as Hermione would hope they would. He would go home, home to the Riddle House. And there Hermione would slam down the trap. Hogwarts defensive spells turned inside out would bind the House. No one could Apparate into the Riddle House, no one could find the Riddle House, no one could reach it except by a few created routes. Now no one would be able to Disapparate from the Riddle House, no one would be able to find the ways out and no one would be able to leave. Dark Lord or not, Voldemort would be a prisoner in his own home.

Now would come the critical research. What are the limits of the prophecy? Only Harry could vanquish Voldemort, but what about imprisoning him in the place he has chosen to enter? Is that beyond the prophecy? Hermione would seek to know.

189

Magical defenses combined with the best of Muggle security, suitably enchanted against Voldemort's magics, would serve to ward her laboratory. Here in the Riddle House Hermione herself would be found. She would not gloat over her victim, for she is not the vanquisher. This is not victory. It is only a series of experiments. Hermione would have to steel herself in order to systematically study and learn and contain her captive.

Like Wormtail before him, Voldemort would become a rat: a lab rat.

There are two magics that Hermione would need to learn about, both poorly understood, and they can only be studied by testing Voldemort.

One is the Dark Arts Voldemort uses to remain alive. What are its limits? Even without finding and destroying his Horcruxes: Can he be killed by bullets, explosives, radiation, hard vacuum, having his body turned inside out?

While he is vulnerable she would place Memory Charms upon

Voldemort, wiping out his knowledge of magic, his years at Hogwarts and other sources of learning. As well, she would make him forget who he is, what he has done and why he did it. He would be not an empty shell, but a bewildered one, wandering through a laboratory hell.

The second magic Hermione would study is Divination, a field that annoys her for its inexactitude. She is no Sybil Trelawney, no occasional prophet who is otherwise a thing of glasses and flummery. Hermione Granger would be systematic and learn its limits. What does "vanquish" mean in the prophecy? What can she do to Voldemort, and how far does the prophecy extend in its protection of him?

These matters she would study, working like a graduate student on her thesis, but with much more care, attention and interest. It would take time, and Hermione would know that she has only so much of it before Voldemort or some hidden follower finds some *190* way for him to escape the prison of his home and flesh.

How long? Months, perhaps a year, while the wizarding and Muggle worlds recover from Voldemort's presence and the passing of his power. Hermione would know that eventually the Ministry of Magic would reassert itself, fear what she is doing and seek to take custody of Voldemort, and then everything would be bollixed up again.

There are plenty of ways she might dispose of the situation. Here's just one, employing a combination of wizarding and Muggle knowledge:

Hermione could turn the entire Riddle House into a Portkey, one that renews itself every day. It might be impossible to transport something as big as a house by Apparition or Floo Powder, but Portkeys travel with the person who uses them. Why not use a big Portkey? She could set it to teleport the House and the person inside it one light year up in the galactic plane. Wizards never seem to have considered the great uses to which the vast emptiness of space could be put in disposing of people. She could take a Time-Turner and set it to turn time back one day at the end of each day. Then she could let it go, leaving her experimental apparatus in place. Voldemort would vanish with his House, still suffering, still memoryless, and passing one light-year per day in airless space where no spells can be said. That day would be endlessly renewed, as a stream of Voldemorts pass in one day up into the sky, triumphant forever, a constellation of his own glory, while inside Voldemort lives forever and a day.

Whether that is the end of things depends on the nature of Time and causality in Potterverse (something Hermione would have studied deeply). If the past is immutable, she and Ron would simply disappear after she had liberated the house-elves completely. It would not be safe for her to be around after the Ministry reasserted itself.

If what has come before is not fixed in stone then Hermione might set into play another plan entirely:

She could finish her research and distill her more-than-a-decade of studies into a small set of teaching books. She would pack them up with a Pensieve, along with a few of Fred and George's more devastating creations. She would kiss Ron goodbye.

Then she would pick up her Time-Turner. And turn, and turn, and turn....

Back to the summer after Voldemort's resurrection, the time when the danger of the Dark Lord has first become real to Harry and his friends. Harry Potter has gone home from Hogwarts to fear what will come and to grow angrier. Young Hermione Granger has gotten off the Hogwarts Express, not knowing that she will be taken later in the summer by the Order of the Phoenix for her own protection. For now, she goes to her Muggle parents, into her Muggle car to be driven to her Muggle home.

From whence she and her parents would disappear. Dumbledore would be alarmed until he read the message left for him and him alone by an older, wiser Hermione Granger. It would be short and to the point, for old Hermione, having seen the wreckage of his plans, no longer trusts Dumbledore with her secrets.

Hermione would face Hermione, girl to woman, both protected against the madness of the meeting by spells the elder had cast. The younger Hermione would look into her own eyes and see pain and knowledge. She would want the knowledge but fear the pain. The older Hermione would want to give the knowledge without the pain.

Here would come another of those unpleasant choices. Some of the pain would have to be handed down if Harry is to be saved. Young Hermione is a follower, and that will never do if the future is not to be as it was. Harry is a hero. He needs guidance and help from his friends, not just his teachers. Above all he must not be permitted to waste this coming year in anger and foolishness. For the sake of Harry and the wizarding and Muggle worlds, Hermione Granger's protective obedience must be broken by the memories of Hermione Granger.

Old Hermione would use Pensieve to give Young Hermione enough memories to know what needs to be done and why. Then she would hand over the books. How could Hermione resist? Four of them would be necessary to contain all needed knowledge. The first would be a spell study guide specifically created to teach in the way Hermione learns best, an accelerated course of study that will give her a few years' learning in a little time. The second book would be an analysis of prophecy and its limits, containing the full prophecy of the Boy Who Lived. The third would be an analysis of the vulnerabilities of Lord Voldemort, and the last a manual of magical strategy and tactics, with a few methods for combining the magical and the mundane. The books would be spelled so that for anyone else they would be dull and uninteresting, the kind of books Hermione would be expected to have and that no one else would look at. The analysis of Voldemort might for irony's sake be disguised as the *Monster Book of Monsters*.

192

There are a lot of things Old Hermione might give Young Hermione: a Time-Turner; a chest modeled on Mad-Eye Moody's, with multiple containers, each full of Fred and George's creations, spelled so that only Hermione could use them safely.

After returning Young Hermione and her parents to their home, Old Hermione would probably seek to undo the damage of the year that is to come. For that, two actions would be needed, the first an act Young Hermione could never do.

Old Hermione would slip through the Ministry of Magic's awesomely pathetic security. Quietly and efficiently she would kill Dolores Umbridge before the Dementors are sent after Harry. Then, making herself appear to be Voldemort, she would fake a very visible raid upon the Hall of Prophecy in such a way that even Cornelius Fudge would have to admit that Voldemort had returned. The news would hit the *Daily Prophet*, and Harry Potter would grow fearful, but not angry.

As to what would happen to Old Hermione, that depends on how causality works. If she can continue to exist, she would probably stay around as some form of guardian angel for her younger self. If not, she would know that, even if Harry fails again there would be a next time, that the cycle of study can continue if need be until eventually they get it right.

Young Hermione Granger would study the books in light of her new memories. She would take them to the Order of the Phoenix, showing them to Dumbledore, as her older self knew she would. Between them they would work out a better course of study for Harry.

When the Weasleys come to the Order Ron would probably notice a glint, a gleam, almost a look of appraisal in Hermione's eyes as she looks at him. What can that girl be thinking of? Barking mad, no doubt of it! Why is she smiling like that?

A few years later Harry Potter would face Lord Voldemort, a wiser Harry Potter who did not lose Sirius or anyone else because Hermione was forewarned. Hermione somehow became more forceful, grown up overnight. Harry Potter would face Lord Voldemort armed magically and conventionally and a bit of both combined. Anticipating each of the Dark Lord's moves, Harry Potter would fulfill the prophecy, destroying his foe once and for all.

Voldemort would come to destruction sulkily, angrily, shouting defiance against Potter and his friends. The Dark Lord would fall, never knowing how lucky he is to lose rather than to triumph forever among the stars.

RICHARD GARFINKLE is the author of two science fiction novels: *Celestial Matters* (which won the 1996 Compton Crook Award for best first novel in science fiction) and *All of an Instant*. At present he is engaged in the more dubious practice of writing non-fiction sci-

193

ence popularization. He lives in Chicago with his wife and children. He credits J. K. Rowling's works with motivating his daughter to excel at reading. This essay is the thanks she gets.

Acknowledgments

Many thanks to the *Harry Potter Lexicon* (http://www.hp-lexicon.org), particularly Michele L. Worley and Steve Vander Ark, and Stephanie Whiteside for their assistance with this manuscript.

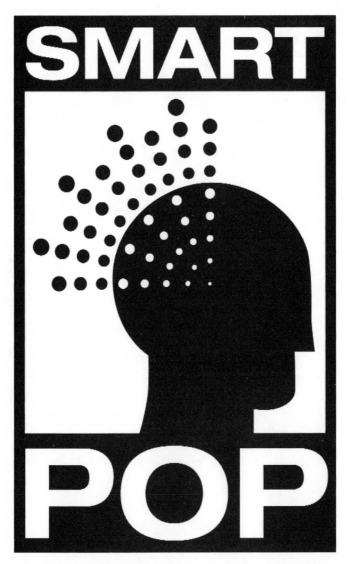

SMART POP CULTURE
SMART POP BOOKS
smartpopbooks.com

Keeping *The Da Vinci Code* fans, conspiracy buffs and puzzle enthusiasts in mind, the mysterious Dr. Ian Browne has woven a story of taut suspense, shocking revelations and a $5,000 prize to the reader who can solve four mind-bending puzzles (among them, who is Dr. Ian Browne?). When Eric San Leté, visiting curator of the Whitney Museum, is found dead, having left only a cryptic message as a clue to his death, Dan Black, professor of modern art, and Saphie Paradise, French exchange student, are sent on a whirlwind adventure to uncover the most profound conspiracy in the history of the human race.

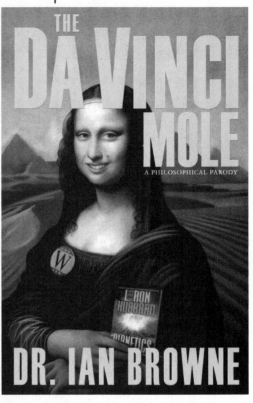

Except for the words, every aspect of *The Da Vinci Mole* is accurate, and it reveals the truths behind some of the great mysteries of the universe, including the secret meaning of Jackson Pollock's paintings, why Intelligent Design is actually correct, definitive proof of the existence of God, the truth behind Area 51, the real rationale for the conservative agenda, the secret plan of the Scientologists and what Karl Rove does in his spare time.

Dr. Ian Browne is the pseudonym for a well-known figure who, for reasons of security, must remain anonymous. His diverse career path has included time as a fighter-jet pilot, professional pool hustler, paid assassin and Bushido master, and he has been rumored to have worked for a clandestine intelligence organization. He has been married to two, and soon three, of the world's most beautiful women. He divides his time between London and Los Angeles.

smartpopbooks.com | BenBella Books

Coming in August 2006

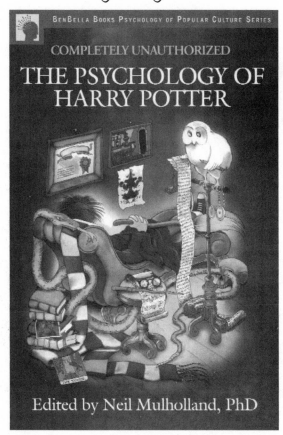

BenBella Books Psychology of Popular Culture Series

COMPLETELY UNAUTHORIZED

THE PSYCHOLOGY OF HARRY POTTER

Edited by Neil Mulholland, PhD

L eading psychologists delve into the psychological brew of Harry Potter in this revealing look at J. K. Rowling's constructed universe, using the characters and their puzzling situations to offer insight into real-world psychology. Designed to appeal to both fans of pop culture and students of psychology, this blend of scholarship and contemporary criticism consists of essays by well-known psychologists. Every major area of psychology is covered as the contributors tackle such heady questions as is Harry a cranky adolescent or suffering from real post-traumatic stress disorder? Is Voldemort evil incarnate or a misguided boy now twisted beyond recognition? And, is Snape treacherous or struggling for redemption?

Now Available

COMPLETELY UNAUTHORIZED

NAVIGATING
THE GOLDEN COMPASS
Religion, Science & Dæmonology in
Philip Pullman's His Dark Materials

Edited by
Glenn Yeffeth

*From the streets of Lyra's Oxford to Dr. Mary
Malone's lab, from the Republic of Heaven to the
harpy-ruled pit of hell,* Navigating the Golden
Compass *examines every aspect of Pullman's
brilliant fantasy.*

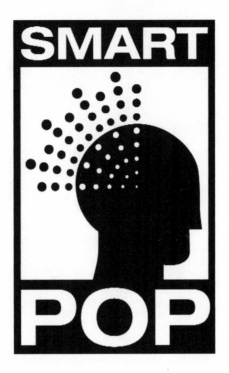